© Anita B. Harmon 2023

All rights reserved. No part of this work may be reproduced, stored in a retrieval system, transmitted in any form or otherwise be copied for public or private use without prior written permission of the author - except for brief quotations embodied in critical articles and reviews. For further information please contact the author by email: anitabharmon@gmail.com

Cover Art: Jesse Hayes

Preface

This is from a journal I kept for three months in 1984, when my best friend, Maggie, was dying in Italy.

Because her death by cancer was so relentless, I kept these notes to clear my head. I wanted to be as fully present with her as I could – as true to as our friendship as I could be, unencumbered by my own horrified reactions.

I hope that no one today has to go through what Maggie went through. I hope pain management is more effective than it was 40 years ago. Because this was not a good death and the only dignity there was came from Maggie herself.

Because I thought this journal was private, I was very frank about my reactions. At the time I wrote these pages it didn't occur to me that they might be helpful to other people faced with a similar situation. People who, in their turn, may be ashamed of their own response to unbearable loss.

Greif, it seems, can be uncivilized.

May

"Are you afraid?" I whisper long distance from London.

Maggie bursts into tears: "I'm sorry, I'm sorry".

Her sobs are wheezes forced out under terrific pressure. She is apologizing for wasting expensive long-distance charges with weeping. Not about the cancer growing in her.

"I'm coming over" is all there is to say.

*

Marco Polo Airport is on strike. Down the steps of the aircraft into an Italian spring - warm and soft after chilly London - we gather, cocktail fashion, around the hold. We have to wait for the pilot and air stewardesses to pull out our luggage. Then we all stagger across the tarmac past a crowd of baggage handlers in blue uniforms, smoking, and staring at the women's legs.

Inside the terminal Marco, Maggie's husband, is not there. I lean against the wall and listen to Italian voices.

People kiss, open doors, smile, haul their luggage and leave.

Marco has asked me not to come.

"Don' come over Anita. Maggie see you - an' she know she is dying."

*

I'd heard from her sister, Jacqueline, that Maggie had bad sciatica. We had met in the Churchyard, with people flowing around us in the after-service organ din. She tells me Maggie's pain had come on gradually from the summer before, getting worse and worse. I had thought nothing of it – never called or wrote. My mother had a bad back and bad backs were nothing special. Just osteopaths and flat-on-your-back for a few frustrating weeks looking at the ceiling.

Then a week ago - the out-of-the-blue phone call from Marco. Maggie has just finished her first chemotherapy treatment. The cancer is terminal, and she is going to die.

It is only when Marco arrives, apologetic, a few minutes late and embraces me that I know I am welcome.

*

Inside the car he tells me about Maggie.

"She hate me. She don' wan' me to do nothing for her. She only listen to the doctors. They all pricks. They don' discover the cancer until it is a big mass, and they can do nothing. They give her the cobalt and chemotherapy to make the cancer smaller. But it bring her down an' make her weak. She lost ten kilos in the 'ospital. She don' eat. Her friends tell me I am cruel to make 'er fight. What kind of friends are these?"

He is so incensed we miss our highway exit twice and nearly have an accident skidding on a sharp bend. Off the main highway we drive through flat farmland. Next to slow moving canals, the earth is sown or fresh-tilled. Pink and lemon farmhouses fade into the evening light. It seems so much more cruel to be dying in spring.

Marco tells me how he collected dew from the grass at first light, for Maggie to drink.

"Is strong in prana, Anita, because it is masculine."

*

We drive into Pordenone where Marco has rented a flat to be near the hospital. It is on the top floor of a square three-storey building with shutters and an orange tiled roof. The balconies flap with washing hung out to dry over geraniums in terracotta pots. We climb slowly up three flights of marble stairs, Marco hauling my suitcase.

Viola, Marco's sister opens the door. She looks tired but smiles her welcome. Behind her and through two more open door ways, I can see Maggie propped up in bed, her black hair against the pillows.

Maggie weeps as I lean down and hold her to me. She doesn't look different, just exhausted. But her body is hot and gritty as if she has sand under her skin. There is a slight smell of vomit.

"I like your hair; it suits you that way." Maggie's first words. I haven't seen her in three years.

Then she speaks to Marco in Italian. He peppers his responses with English.

"Bu' what you want? Strawberries? Bread and butter? What? I make food for you, bu' you don' eat it."
"I don't know - I don't know."
They shout at one another. She gets out of bed, pushes him aside and hobbles into another room. I follow and sit next to her on a couch. She weeps again and I put my arm around her.

"Am I really ill do you think?"

"Yes. You are very ill indeed."
"I don't feel ill. I felt worse when I got the chicken pox from the children two years ago. I feel as if I am having a nervous breakdown."

Marco comes in. He squats in front of Maggie and takes her feet. He speaks quietly and smiles. They laugh. Then he goes out to make her some orange juice.

*

I go into the kitchen to find a vase for the freesias I bought this morning from a London stall. Maggie's father used to grow them in winter for the spring market.

As soon as they were in bud, Mrs Adey would bring them home from the greenhouses and set them in glass jam jars. When they began to open, she made them into thin bunches with wads of wet cotton wool and an elastic band. With quick hands she worked with her eyes squinted against the smoke from her cigarette hanging from her lips - an inch of ash at the end.

*

Me and Maggie. Maggie and me on the hearthrug. The scent of freesias mingled with the smell of coal from the fire on dark February evenings.

*

On the way back to Maggie and Marco's room, I pass Viola as she opens the door to where she has been sleeping. Inside, the lights are on and Maggie's two little girls, Daisy and Chloe, are sitting up in a huge double bed. They look at me with curious, bright eyes. With no Italian I can only smile at them, my hands full of freesias.

*

Maggie pushes the covers aside and sits on the edge of the bed. She hangs her head and hums, an old habit of hers when she was frustrated.

Hummm, hummm.

Then she looks up, humming, at the window beside her bed. It is too high up to see anything but a bit of sky. She pushes herself onto her good leg, grabs the window sill for balance and starts to faint.

"Marco! Marco!"

In her panic, she has forgotten that I am right next to her. He rushes in from the kitchen and I leap out of the way. He helps her sit down on the bed again.

"You mus' take it slow." He puts his arm around her. "You don' eat an' it make you weak."

Marco goes back to the kitchen to cook lunch with Viola and the little girls. I give Maggie my arm and support her into the bathroom. She walks with a strange rolling gait - as if she has just disembarked from a ship after years at sea.

The bathroom is bright with sunshine that sparkles on the porcelain. Next to the toilet, a door to a tiny balcony is open onto a slash of spring light and the chatter of sparrows. I drag a chair in front of the basin and help her to sit.

Hmmmm Hmmmm.

Maggie sigh-hums. She rests her forearms on the side of the basin and her hands dangle at the wrists into the bright sun-lit well. She fumbles the plug into place and turns on the taps. They gush and froth as she unhooks a flannel from the wall. She soaps it with slow, circular movements. I don't know what to do so I perch next to her on the bidet. She turns off the taps and soaps her face, neck and arms. Gradually, she livens up. She rinses off and leans over the sink. Drops and rivulets of water flash in the sun. Marco pops his head round the door.

"You wan' some clean things?"

"Yes. And get me some clean socks. I'm going to do my feet. They must stink." She sounds cross - disgusted. Marco ducks back out.

"Pass me some powder, Anita."

When I help her on with her clean knickers, I look at her bottom. The skin around her buttock and groin is burnt to a purplish brown, like a bad grape.

There is no hair on your fanny!

"I know. It all fell out after the cobalt. They said my hair might fall out too. But I might be lucky. Sometimes it doesn't."

She is cold. I help her into a clean nightie and button it up. She is tiring fast. I kneel down and peel off her socks. To my surprise her feet are bandaged around the arch and have bright purple marks between the toes.

"What happened to your feet?"

"Oh I don't know. They opened them up to look at the lymph glands or something.'" She is impatient. She doesn't want to know what is done to her or why.

"But your toes..."

"That was for the Xray. They injected purple dye into the veins. It was agony." She washes her toes in the bidet, being careful not to get the bandages wet. "They are going to operate. When they finish the chemotherapy. When the tumor is smaller."

*

I ask Marco later if this is true - if they are going to operate.

"No. They think in the beginning they can operate, but they can do nothing. We 'ave to tell 'er soon."

I need to sort out my feelings. I think I am very angry.
But my reaction rushes backwards in time.

Maggie and I were so often in trouble as children, so I
can't sort it out emotionally - this difference between
adult disapproval and dying.

I wander into the living room and my put-up bed to
wait for lunch. This is my bedroom until Viola and the
girls leave. It is a big room with a marble floor and glass
doors that open onto a balcony. It has a three-piece
suite, and a naked light bulb hangs from the ceiling.
There are no carpets and I hate it.

Chloe, stands by the door. She is eight, with thick red hair
and a freckled face. I draw her picture and call her over.

"Chloe, comme si dice?"

She comes across the room and looks at my picture.
"Sol." She grins.
I hand her my pen and together we start a dictionary.
She draws a star. "Stella," and I draw the moon. "Luna."

Our involvement soon attracts Daisy, Maggie's older
daughter. Daisy is ten, blonde and skinny. She takes
over and squabbling, they teach me Italian.

*

After lunch Maggie is dozing. The weather is fine - so I
suggest to Marco that we go and look for a park.

"This place is a shit-hole."

"But surely there must be somewhere. The children need to get out. They are both at a very loose end."

"Okay Anita." Marco goes to check with Maggie to see if she minds being left.

"Oh no. They need the exercise. I'll be all right with Viola."

Outside, the sun is warm so we don't need coats. The birds are noisy, nest-building. And as we drive off, I am so eager to get away I'm ashamed. I don't want to feel as if I am escaping from prison. In town Marco rolls down the window.

"Per favore, Signora, dove una gardina publica?"

A woman with a shopping basket, her cardigan loose around her shoulders, stands in the sun. She points down the road. There is a park and it is close by.

We find it easily and walk towards the entrance, lizards whisking out of our shadows.

Inside swans' blaze in and out of the sun, their wings set to scatter the ducks. Marco and I stroll along the gravel paths through long grass, rank with daisies and yellow buttercups. We crack jokes and laugh together. He needs this freedom - time away from cancer.

We come upon an old carriage house, where a Grey Crow is cooped into a small cage. In the gloom, it hops incessantly back and forth between two perches, less than a foot apart.

"They keep it because it is rare. In Italy, the country people, they keep anything like that."

*

Marco decides that we'll get some gelatti.

We leave the park and run across the road to the car. Daisy's hand, cupped in mine for safety, is a fist.

The café is cool and shaded under a canvas awning, with wicker chairs and green, linen table cloths. We gloat over our ice creams. Marco, glad to provide me with pleasure, enjoys me enjoying myself. We watch Daisy and Chloe play. They run up and down some broad stone stairs that lead to a balcony.

They peep through the balustrade at us. Their fringes hang in their eyes.

"I've never been in love," remarks Marco.

*

When we get back, we have been away for too long. Maggie holds her arms out to Marco and her hands hang limp from the wrists, her elbows bent. She looks like a defeated baby.

*

Mateo, Marco's twin brother has arrived to take Viola and the little girls back home. Even though Mateo is a mirror to Marco, he is bigger and more charismatic, with all the confidence of the handsome, unmarried, Latin male. They live 50 miles away in Oriago. Daisy and Chloe must go back to school.

Maggie is complaining. They all group around her, Marco, Mateo, Viola, and I sit out of the way in a corner, as they reason with her - their faces sad and earnest. Suddenly Maggie speaks in English:

"Si, but I have to have the operation, no?"

Marco is rough. "There is no operation. They can do nothing." He speaks as if it must be obvious to an idiot.

Maggie bursts into tears and covers her face with her hands.

"Let me face the facts." She rolls, sobbing, over onto her side and hides under the bed clothes.

Marco leaves the room.

Viola and Mateo lean over to comfort her After a while she comes out and Mateo talks to her.

He goes on and on, with sad-faced asides from Viola, who nods in agreement and echoes what he is saying.

I can't understand, but know it is a lecture and wish it would stop. Finally, he looks across at me:

"It is the will to live, da is important, Eh Anita."

Instantly I am enraged. But he doesn't notice and carries on. When he has finished he goes out of the room, followed by Viola, so they can pack and prepare to leave with the little girls.

I move over to Maggie.

"I don't feel ill," she says again. "I feel as if I am having a nervous breakdown."

I say nothing.

"I have to face the fact."

"What fact?"

"That this cancer is going to be difficult to cure."

We sit quiet. The room fills with shadow. Sounds of voices, laughing and talking, reach us from the kitchen.

Maggie wants to get up. She walks with her crab gait into the living room and sits on the couch. She is cold, so I fetch pillows and blankets, to wrap her up.

"I must eat."

"What would you like?"

"I don't know. I've just got no appetite. My mouth feels awful."

"What about fresh-squeezed oranges? It would make your mouth feel fresh."

Hmmmm.

I go and place the order with Marco who is relaxing in the kitchen, drinking wine with Mateo. Viola is getting odds and ends into a cardboard box. She is smiling. It will soon be time to leave.

"Maggie wants some orange juice."

They scatter. Viola looks in the fridge for fresh oranges, Marco digs for the squeezer, and Mateo gets out of the way. The kitchen has just enough room for a round table and four chairs, with a fridge in the corner and a few shelves. I leave them to it and go back to Maggie. She is nauseous and faint.

"Get Marco."

Her voice is sharp with fear. I call out, and both Marco and Mateo come in and sit on either side of her, identical as book ends, their voices gentle. Chloe is sent in by Viola to say goodbye. It is time for her to go. Maggie smiles at her and starts to say something, but breaks into tears again.

"Please take me back to bed."

She leaves the room, swathed in blankets and supported by the brothers.

Chloe runs from window to window and drops all the shutters. They bang down, one by one, and when the room is completely dark - she leaves.

*

"Go an' have some wine, Anita." Marco nudges me towards the kitchen. "I'm goin' to get some pizza,"

I go into the kitchen and sit down at the table where Viola and Mateo are talking, eyeball to eyeball. Mateo breaks off and turns to me.

"It is important not to baby Maggie."

This is too much.

"It is more important not to make her feel responsible for her state."

Barely under control, my voice shakes with rage.
In the following silence, I go back into the living room. Someone has put up the shutters again.

*

Marco left early this morning to go to work. He has been off for five months, but every so often, he has to report back to wheedle more time.

Rosie, a nurse arrives. I open the door for her and she bounces past me into Maggie's room.

She comes every day to give Maggie a vitamin injection and she does it for nothing.

"In Italy, no one does anything for nothing Anita."

Maggie rubs her thumb and fingers together in the universal gesture for money.

"She must really like you then."

"In hospital I shit bright green all over the bed. It was revolting. Rosie cleaned me up. When I could walk, I'd go to the nurses station in the middle of the night, hanging on to the wall calling, Rosie, Rosie.

I feel a stab of jealousy. It was Rosie who was there, not me.

"Giourno Signora," she smiles as I stand aside for her at the door.

Maggie lies on her side, while Rosie administers the shot. She talks all the time, and Maggie replies, laughing, in Italian. They mimic one another, remembering Maggie's distress in hospital: Rosie, Rosie.

*

After Rosie leaves, Maggie asks: "How is your mother?"

I prepare to entertain: "She went through the windscreen of Granny's car - They had an accident last Christmas."

"Your poor mother! Is she all right?"

Maggie is laughing already. My grandmother's bad driving is legendary.

"Well. Granny was taking Frank and his mother home. Mummy was over for Christmas and so she went with them. It was night, and Granny, pulled out to overtake but blinded by oncoming headlights, when she pulled in again she forgot to straighten out. She crashed into a three-foot thick, Guernsey granite wall.

Mummy hit the windscreen and Frank and his mother ended up in a heap on the back seat floor. The first thing Granny said was: Who hit us? She was really pissed off."

Maggie begins to laugh in earnest.

"They are all taken to hospital for shock and cuts from flying glass. Mummy has blood all over her best fur coat. Poor old Mrs. Boogough was quivering with the palsy and Frank, to every one's astonishment, starts singing dirty sea shanties at the top of his voice. Granny, of course, is completely unscathed."

Maggie's mouth goes down at the corners, and she makes her familiar gasping sound, her eyes closed. I laugh too, the tears rolling down my face.

"When they finally all get back home, Granny calmly goes upstairs to get changed for bridge. "But I can't let them down dear, they must have a four.'"

Maggie bangs the covers with her hand. "My God," she gasps, "you can't let down a bridge party, it's worse than being excommunicated!"

*

When Granny throws one of her afternoon fours, Maggie and me, we creep into the kitchen to wait for the tea trolley to come out of the dining room. When the door opens, we hear trills of laughter over the rumble of the wheels: *Darling, how perfectly dreadful!*

We are surreptitious because we don't want to go in and be polite. We just want to finish off the cheese scones and remains of homemade cake. If we're caught we go in together.

Here she is, my Grandmother says, her face happy. *And this is Margaret. They are inseparable.*

Maggie is behind me, balanced on one sun-browned, sandaled foot. She stands head down, so that her grey-blue eyes are hidden by her straight, black fringe. Cigarette smoke curls and hazes the afternoon sun.

My goodness, how you have grown. Do you still ride? And how is Margaret?

The old ladies soon forget us. They lean across the table at one another, and we slip away into the early evening - duty done.

My childhood begins with Maggie.

One day, after tea, my Grandmother took me by the hand and led me across the lane to Mrs. Adey's house. I had just been sent over from London, because my mother has gone into hospital. I am seven years old.

We go through a tall wooden gate labeled Malamir and walk up a gravel path. Mrs. Adey comes out to greet us with Maggie and her sister, Jacqueline, in tow.

This grubby little girl wants someone to play with, says my Grandmother.

*

Maggie is bright this morning - ready to enjoy herself and take command.

"Now, Anita, I know you want to go and do some shopping and you must telephone Andy. He'll want to know how you are."

There is no phone and I haven't had time to find one. Time telescopes itself around Maggie, so that there is no time at all - yet nothing to do.

"I must get to the bank as well, and cash some traveler's checks. I want to give you something towards my keep."

"No, no," Maggie and Marco both chorus, looking dismayed.

"At least I want some lira in my pocket and change for the pay phone."

"Ah. You will need gettones. The bank will have them."

After breakfast, I go into her bedroom to help her dress.

"My things are all in there," she says, and points to a big wardrobe next to the bed. She unbuttons her nightie and I open the doors.

"I'll wear my red cardigan." She smiles, her face betraying pride.

I look in the wardrobe for it. It is scarlet wool of thick mohair. Knit with big shoulder pads to give it shape and fall, it gives off a poppy-colored halo of fluff. As I take it off its special, padded hanger, I can feel its softness and smell Rive Gauche - Maggie's perfume.

"Maybe when she is dead…" a voice whispers in my head

"Oh good, you've found it".

Horrified at myself, I help her into her clothes.

Everything is too big for her.

You can't go to church in those tights!

Why not?

You just can't? Maggie is near to tears.

Maggie has come to watch me dress. I am over for the Christmas holidays, and all that winter the school fashion in London has been for brightly colored tights under kilts. I have just put on my favorite scarlet pair. I am thirteen and Maggie is twelve.

But I wear them to school all the time! Everyone wears them.

It doesn't matter. You can't wear them here.

Too bad!

I run out of the bedroom and down the stairs to join Granny in the dining room. I know Maggie won't dare say anything in front of my Grandmother - who couldn't care less about what I wear - as long as I am tidy. And, I also know, Maggie won't refuse to come with us in the car — because if she walks to church alone, she will be late.

Maggie hangs her head, her face red with humiliation, impotent tears of rage in her eyes.

Come along you two, cries Granny, as she takes off for the back door, and heads up the garden path to the garage in her usual hurry-up trot, gloves and prayer books in hand - hand bag clamped under her elbow. I stick close behind her with Maggie a lagging third. We climb into the Morris Minor and drive up the lane to Granny's usual chatter.

Oh look, there's dear Colonel Lawon. He gave me some Brussels sprouts from his garden last week – big fat ones.

We park the car and follow her through Norman arch of St Martins Church, Maggie utterly silent. I stand tall, and Maggie, I know without looking, is making herself look as small as possible.

Her grown-up sister sings in the choir and my scarlet tights will not go unnoticed. Sunday lunch is going to be hell for Maggie as she is teased and grumbled at by her family who think I am no better than I should be and the scarlet tights are going to prove it, once and for all.

Granny assumes her pious scuttle as we make for her pew at the front of the congregation. I walk down the aisle behind her, well aware of the many pairs of eyes riveted on my scarlet legs. I slow down so everyone can have a good look.

But what I didn't expect was that Maggie catches up and stalks at the same royal pace by my side, her nose in the air. Which is why I love her better than I love myself. Even though I can be so spiteful to her.

Marco helps Maggie down the stairs. She descends with care, humping her body on her good leg. Her scarlet shoulders sink lopsided into another sunny day. The gardens are full of lilac, wisteria and forsythia that hang with the weight of their blooms.

Our first stop in Pordenone is the health food shop. Maggie wants to come in with us so I help her out of the car onto the pavement. Heavy and warm on my arm, she stands crouched in the scent of yeast and dried apricots, looking about her. An assistant comes forward with a chair and Maggie sits. She looks down and admires the floor.

"These tiles must be at least a hundred years old'."

All the goods are in hessian sacks and have to be weighed and packaged separately. It takes a long time. Marco and the assistant keep up a constant flow of chatter, while she puts it all together.

Maggie keeps shifting from one buttock to another. The conversation is irritating her.

"I think we should take you back now," I tell her. But she is stubborn.

"No. We must finish. I'll be all right."

The rush around Pordenone to finish our errands as fast as we can makes us silent and grim. Maggie cannot keep still, and grimaces if the car jerks or stops. When we get home, Marco helps her out of the car. She nearly faints and has to sit down again, with her head between her knees. Marco empties the car of groceries, and dashes up ahead of us with armfuls of bags. In the flat, she collapses sideways onto the bed and curls up with her eyes closed.

I help Marco to put away the groceries and make lunch, and later when we have eaten, Maggie feels better. She rolls onto her back, and bends her legs, so that her knees are near her face. She crosses her hands over her shins, and in this fetal position, finds relaxation. She looks up, out of the window, at the sky.

I climb next to her onto the bed. This time I lie with my head on a pillow next to her feet.

This way I can see her face.

*

On wet afternoons we would often lie nose-to-tail like this, reading as the rain soothed the window. We'd get warm under Maggie's blue silk eiderdown. Sometimes, I'd buy us a box of chocolates to gorge.

Phooagh! You've farted. My god what a pong!

I put on my best haughty look. *I don't know what you mean.*

It's going green under here, she'd insist, peering under the quilt, and slamming it back into place, her face appalled.

And I'd giggle too, unable to resist her clowning – our satisfaction with one another, complete.

*

Ending and beginning have run together – the days are fallen out of order - intensities of being from past and present overlapping – like waves. The afternoon is quiet and I doze off.

As far as I know, Maggie stays awake for when I open my eyes, she hasn't moved. She still lies against the pillows, looking up at the sky. The light from the window shines blue on her face.

"I don't think I want my leg cut off, because the cancer would probably come back in five years anyway."

Over on the dressing table, there is a big manila envelope with 'X-ray' stenciled on it. I have noticed it before but, so far, I haven't looked.

"Can I look at your X-rays?"

"Yes, of course."

I pull out several large negatives and a whole lot of small ones. I hold them up, one by one, to the window.

The small ones seem to have been taken from the top of her head. I don't understand them at all. The large ones are of her pelvis, and on one of them is a curve of red arrows. It outlines a pale mass that takes up a third of her pelvic cavity. I put them away and lie down on Marco's bed. She is dozing now and I don't want to disturb her.

I drift into a day dream: I dream up a swarm of tiny fish — make them swim, from my pelvis into hers. They tease and pull at the cancer, in the way of fish, and reduce it bite by bite.

*

This morning I look out of my window and see mountains hung across the sky. They are so tall that at first, I think they are clouds.

*

Maggie wakes up tired. She doesn't want to talk or be entertained. I mooch around the flat at a loose end. On the kitchen balcony the sun is warm. I lean over the parapet and watch some children, off from school. They have organized a game of football. Two dogs hang about, wagging their tails. I wash some clothes in the bathroom sink, with sunshine splashes on my bare feet.

*

We have to get Maggie up. She must go to the hospital to have the stitches removed from her feet. I have no idea why they cut the tops of her feet open. The stitches stick up like black thorns.

The way into the hospital is through an archway guarded by a man in uniform.

Marco leans out of the car window:

"Reparto di Oncologia?"

The guard points the way to the side of the hospital.

Patients in pajamas and dressing gowns are scattered about about the lawns in hospital chairs. Personnel flap by in open white coats.

I support Maggie through dusty glass doors.

A vivid rectangle of light stops dead just beyond our feet. In the dark, beyond our sun dazzled eyes an empty desk, surrounded by pillars, waits in the gloom. Some rearrangement or enlarging of the hospital has rendered it obsolete. A small lift at the back makes a crowd when the three of us enter with two more people.

We get off on the seventh floor at the Reparto di 'Oncologia, where two nuns on their knees are washing the wide lino passage that leads from the lift to the ward. They will not let us pass. We have to wait for the floor to dry and there are no chairs. Maggie, bent into a crouch, leans against the wall for support. Next to us on the wall a white plaster Virgin Mary holds out her arms.

*

Maggie limps into her old room for a chat – a room with three beds. By the window, lies a young girl, her head swathed in a white scarf. On the opposite wall, a woman in a black wig, a huge dressing on her left breast, talks with her husband. Maggie declines several invitations to sit down and directs most of her conversation to the girl, who smiles.

Rosie, the nurse, sticks her head round the door with a flow of Italian. Time to have the stitches out. We limp up the hall into the Out-Patients room, Marco flirting with Rosie over Maggie's head.

On the sunny side of the hospital, the light catches the sinks and chrome taps - makes the metal implements blatant. The trolley with tweezers, scissors and scalpels rattles over to Maggie who cannot get comfortable on the examination table. Rosie is patient and waits until Maggie is ready and still. Then, with cotton swabs of iodine and small scissors, she performs the simple operation. One stitch gets stuck and as Rosie tugs, the skin on Maggie's foot stretches into an impossible peak.

*

Maggie feels like a drive, so Marco takes us out of the town and into the farmland. He finds a dirt track between newly-ploughed fields full of stones. Some fields are un-ploughed - lush with spring grass that hisses in the breeze. Marco drives carefully so as not to bounce Maggie about.

*

In the bathroom, I sit on the toilet and fold Maggie's pajamas into my lap. Marco, in a chair pulled up close to the bath, leans over to wash her. Maggie's thighs are wasted away with a large triangular gap at the top, under her fanny, which is bald and burnt dark brown. She smiles and gives sighs of pleasure. She teases Marco in Italian. In return, he flicks her nipples.

It is late and a squall of rain hammers the roof.

*

This morning I lean out of my window onto a wet world. At the foot of the building, rings expand on the puddles in musical time to Sunday bells and sparrow-cheeps. Rain hushes steadily onto leaves.

In the kitchen I breakfast with Marco on muesli and honey from the health food shop.

"My stomach is an aching balloon."

"You mus' chew your food forty times. At the homeopathic medicine shop, the man tell me to chew each mouthful forty times, and then you never get indigestion."

I chew the muesli and count to myself. Marco does the same and we sit in silence over our cud, eyes fixed on an imaginary horizon. Maggie limps in and uses the door jamb for support.

"My God, I can hear you in the bedroom. It's disgusting."

I splutter with laughter. She is hungry this morning and eats corn-flakes, yogurt and toast, while Marco and I beam at her over our ruminating mouths.

"We could go up into the mountains," says Marco.

*

After we are dressed and packed into the car we drive off. Maggie takes out the map and they both quarrel in Italian over the direction we should take. Marco, who is tired, begins to lose his temper. His voice rises and he chops his hands through the air.

"They can't be that difficult to find," I say from between them on the back seat, "they are big enough. Why don't you just take any road that goes up, and why don't I massage your shoulders?"

"Yes, why don' you?" agrees Marco, and calms down immediately.

Marco's muscles are tense and rigid with knots around the shoulder-blades and a big lump on the side of his neck. He has borne the burden of Maggie's illness for months.

*

We find a climbing road, steep and drenched - half-hidden in fog. Trees and grass fade in and out of tatters in the clouds and the sharp green of late spring floats behind the smoke. For a moment, we are in the clear, loomed over by a green hill covered in white boulders, and then it is gone. We pass through a small, wet village where a tree grows out of the church belfry.

Maggie begins to hurt, so we turn back.

*

In the bedroom I undress her and tuck her in. "I'm cold," she says, curls onto one side, shivers.

I get blankets from my bed and make her a hot water bottle. Then I lie next to her, nose to tail again, with a pack of cards to play patience.

Marco goes to visit the kids.

"I liked my grandfather."

"Yes. I remember him. He'd arrange a long sausage of coins in his hand, and then he'd ask you if you wanted a copper one or a silver one."

"He used to hang about the green houses irritating the workmen and I followed him for company."

"I suppose he was retired."

"Yes, he must have been."

"Your grandmother was a bitch."

"God yes." Maggie hitches herself up into a sitting position. "We've got millions of relatives from her, but we don't know who they are, thank God. Sometimes, I think I'm like her, and I worry."

"No you are not. You've got much more love in you."

*

We climb into Mrs Vinning's house through the toilet window and crack her lavatory pan. The Adey's are away for a few days and Maggie is staying with her grandmother, who has locked her out. Maggie is only allowed in at certain times and is not allowed a key.

The lavatory has to be replaced and the whole family, the Adey's and the Vinnings, are ranked against us for costing them money. After a huge row are sent in to apologize. Maggie's grandmother sits on a chair in the best parlor, used only for guests - or at Christmas. Maggie's grandfather stands behind her – like a Victorian portrait. I had thought to bring along a bunch of daffodils as reparation. I whip them out from behind my back but she just gives me a frigid stare and refuses to touch them.

*

"Your Granzy was nice."

I remind Maggie of her other grandmother, the one we liked to visit on the Forest Road. "I thought she was a witch, because she had a crystal ball and so many cats."

"When she was young, she and her husband ditched Dad and Uncle Cyril and went to Persia. That's where all those lovely old rugs came from."

"Really? I'd never thought to wonder - but of course she had Persians all over the place. They must have been worth a fortune - soaked in cat's pee."

"Quite." Maggie puts on her mock-disgusted face. Which is a frown and a long look down her nose, with her jaw dropped open under pursed lips. I laugh.

"That's why Dad grew up with a Guernsey accent. He and Cyril were left with country people. They never forgave her for it."

"Is that why your father was so sensitive about you ruining the family name? "

This was Mr. Adey's famous complaint : Famous, because she so often ruined the family name over the strangest things: Like the time he discovered that Maggie, who hated breakfast, used to shove her toast into the thick ivy growing along the lanes, on her way to school.

"Uncle Syd has ruined the family name too. He worked his whole life for the States of Guernsey and when he died, they found he had cheated them of thousands. No one knew how. They still can't balance his books. Mum and Dad always thought his children had done remarkably well!"

Maggie is silent for a while.

"They never told me when Dad was dying. They always treated me like a baby. They wanted to protect me I suppose. I thought he was all right and then I got the phone call. I told them:

"But I was there for six months and he was fine. Why didn't you tell me he was ill again?" They never told me anything. They still don't'."

"They excluded you. I remember. They always disapproved of you."

"Yes." She sighs. "Jacqueline was the good one."

*

Maggie the second child, without the grace to be born a boy, was conceived by mistake at the end of the war. Her sister Jacqueline six years older than us, is her mother's darling.

Maggie was bought up to stay out of the way.

Stop that Margaret, her father growls.

It is teatime and Maggie is sucking her thumb. Irritated by her babyishness, he glares at her over the daily loaf of bread he cuts for the family, every teatime.

*

Tears wet Maggie's face.

"I am so afraid I won't see home again - the sea and the wind coming in over the rocks. Around here the sea is like a piss-pot."

I stroke her head with my fingertips and brush the hair out of her eyes. There are no words. Only the clear sea of home will answer, rolling in waves - knocking pebbles together - where the gulls cry and wheel out from the cliffs, gliding on the wind.

Her back against the white pillows, her eyes on the sky outside the window:

"Have they given me a time limit?' 'Two or three months for instance?"

There is no pause, before I say "No", with seamless confidence.

Appalled, I pick up the playing cards and arrange a fresh hand of patience, one slow card on top of the other. At this moment of truth my mind has presented me with a blank. As if I am asleep and I must force myself awake. As if I have spoken out of a dream, where no matter how fast I try to run, I can only go in agonizing slow motion.

I have just lied to her for the first time in my life.

"I feel bad about not being able to look after the children."

"It must make you feel guilty."

"Yes it does. But I don't want them to see me this way and to tell the truth, I don't think they want to see me this way either, especially Daisy. She must think I am getting better."

Marco comes home, and, after supper, we all play cards.

Maggie wins easily. With three of us on the bed it creaks and sways. We all get wild and hysterical.

"Fuckin' shit," swears Marco as the bed groans and Maggie wins again. She miscounts her points and gives herself more than she has won.

"Just because you've got cancer, doesn't mean we're going to let you get away with cheating at cards."

She laughs and points upwards. "You wait till I'm up there."

*

Later, in the bath, I hear her sobs in the bedroom, and Marco's voice, soothing. I look down at my fat, soapy body with loathing.

I can give her all my money, I can give her my home, she can even have my husband Andy, if she wants him, but I can't give her my health.

Rain hammers on the roof.

*

This morning, Maggie wakes me up with a glass of home-made banana milk shake in her hand. Marco has made it for her breakfast and there is some left over.

"Here you are Anita. "It's delicious."

I make a face at it.

"Excuse me!" She hobbles back into the kitchen with a grin on her face.

*

Maggie washes her hair at the bathroom sink. When she is done she sits on the side of her bed to comb it out. Instead of sliding through, the comb comes away from her head with her wet, tangled hair stuck in the teeth. It is beginning to come out. She falls on her side, curls up, and cries. I put my arms around her.

*

Mateo arrives, to take me out to the telephone. Because there is no phone in the flat, and I have to go out to call home. But no one answers - so instead he takes me for a Cappuccino.

"I need women, bu' I canno' stand to get married. Pretty soon they wan' you should marry them."

He makes a reigning in motion. "Then they wan' your soul."

His English is terrible, much worse than Marco's. But I get the picture.

"Then no woman can win with you: she is either too dependent or too strong. Either way, you complain we cut your balls off."

He laughs. "An 'den there is nothing to fuck with."

"Have you ever been in love?" I am curious after Marco's comment at the Gelateria.

"No. But sometime I feel I could be in love with all women. Dey all got something."

It is odd being with twins. I am always comparing them in a way I wouldn't if they were merely brothers. Mateo looks older and seems more rugged and down-to-earth, as if he has decided to be the practical one. Marco seems smaller, more finely made - the one who is mystical.

"I don' need to marry. I learn from Marco an' Maggie. I don' wan' the struggle."

*

I dream that Maggie and I sail to an island of sand and rock. We disembark to go and explore. We walk on the sand - but Maggie is on quicksand. I beg her to get out and come over to where I am. But she is stubborn and insists on walking through it. She is in great danger. But to my joy, she makes it through, and sinks only as far as her knees.

*

I wake up and join the two brothers in the kitchen for breakfast, determined that we should go out.

"Maggie was in all day yesterday."

"All right, Anita," agrees Marco.

She is in a foul temper this morning. She hasn't slept well, and both she and Marco look pasty and grim.

"I think I might be getting my period." she complains. "I got one after the cobalt treatment. It was agony, and it went on for ages."

"Do you feel like going out?"

"Yes. I want to buy some flowers for Rosie today. I want to give her something."

"We get some cassettes too," says Marco. "Then we can 'ave some good music."

"And we have to get some food."

Maggie goes into the bathroom to wash before getting dressed. When she comes out, she goes into her bedroom, lies on the bed and weeps.

"My hair is really coming out."

It is true. In the bathroom her hair brush is full of black, silky hair and the sink is cracked with it. I cover her with a blanket.

"I'm cold."

I go into the kitchen and make her a hot water bottle for the journey into town.

*

In the flower shop Maggie chooses roses for Rosie. The shop owner gives me a pink one.

"They never do that for me. I jus' don' understand it."

Mateo smiles into my eyes.

*

Marco and Mateo go on a whirlwind tour of the market, and get back to the car laden with vegetables, fruit, fish and chicken. I stay with Maggie. She is still depressed and bad-tempered. We decide it is best to go back home.

*

The brothers prepare chicken and vegetables, working together, speaking in Italian and broken English, for my benefit. The sun streams through the open French windows from the kitchen balcony. Lunch is delicious, and we eat together in the kitchen, while Maggie rests, alone, in the bedroom.

Later in the afternoon, Mateo leaves and, soon after, Rosie arrives. After Maggie's injection, they both come into the kitchen, and I make coffee. Maggie has given her the roses and they sit down at the table for a long chat. I don't understand any of it, of course, but stay and watch. Maggie is animated and she and Rosie laugh like conspirators. I am over my jealousy and join in with smiles and find some sugar for Rosie's coffee.

"Grazie signora."

*

In the early evening, Maggie wants to go out again, so Marco drives us to the same place we went to a few days ago after she had her stiches out of her feet.

"It's amazing that the corn grows so well with all these stones."

In places, the earth is white with them like some kind of guano. In the distance, a tractor bubbles, past turning over new hay while two men follow with pitchforks.

The smell reaches us on the warm air through the open car windows. Maggie sits quite still - her profile dark against the light outside. Two magpies fly past.

"One for sorrow, two for joy," says Marco.

Elated by the moment, I quote from Monty Python.

'..this parrot is deceased, dead, gone before. This parrot is singing with the choirs' invisibule, pushing up the daisies....No, no, it's just pining for the fiords...

Maggie gasps for breath through her laughter. It is only afterwards that I realize what an incredibly tactless passage to use.

*

We stop outside a deserted, pink villa, left over from some past, done on a grander scale - set back from the road, behind an overgrown lawn covered in dandelion clocks. Their seeds float in and out of the shadows, under trees gone to the wild and the beginnings of night-fall. We peer through the wrought iron gates - their pillars topped by seated lions – at the wooden shutters closed onto crumbling balconies. A shrine with a wooden Madonna and child, draped in white linen and a rosary stands next to the gates. She looks very masculine.

"I think it must be Saint Christopher, carrying Christ."

"No," says Marco. "Not here. The country people would not take care of St. Christopher."

"Maybe it was Saint Christopher to begin with and got turned into Mary. After all Jesus is on her shoulder."

*

We prepare supper to the Mamas and the Papas.

...and Monday morning, Monday morning couldn't guarantee, that Monday evening you would still, be here, with me.

I peel apples for apple sauce, and Marco deep-fries pieces of fish and octopus. Maggie who has had a nap comes in and criticizes every move we make.

The fat isn't hot enough for the fish. The chair is in the wrong place for her. The saucepan handle is over the flame.

"Rompe cojone!" Marco reaches for his crotch. "You break my balls."

Marco washes up afterwards and I dry. Outside, a puppy plays under a streetlamp, and I throw the left-over meat from this morning's broth. The puppy takes the prize through a hole under a hedge, its little body serious with the weight.

At bed time, Maggie lies naked and thin in the bath and we sing Christmas carols.

"Do you remember when you sang the Gloria in Excelsis chorus all by yourself?"

"God, yes. The choir was supposed to sing the chorus alone and I didn't know. I launched in at the top of my voice. I was so loud I didn't hear that none of the congregation was singing."

She chuckles. "You sang out of tune, too."

*

For once I am the first up. Maggie waves from her bed. The day is overcast, and the curtains drawn, so that she is in a pool of gloom. I mouth and sign so as not to wake Marco on his camp bed.

"Would you like some breakfast?"

She nods vigorously and mouths back. "Half a glass of carrot juice."

In the kitchen, I feel snotty and take some vitamin C. Maggie comes limping in.

"Cut the carrots on the board, Anita, or you'll cut yourself."

Marco comes in and hugs us both. He is congested as well.

Maggie's scalp is sore and her hair is coming out in earnest. She looks up at us with tears in her eyes:

"At least I'm not having a nervous breakdown."

*

Maggie is comfy in the passenger seat, so we decide to go up into the mountains again. The sun comes out. Maggie and Marco quarrel over the map, but soon we are on the right road and heading for the skyline, reared up over our heads.

We climb through little villages with their faded houses, one church, and one cafe.

Higher up we stop at another shrine. This one is definitely a Madonna and Child, in bas relief, with a vase of wild flowers set before her. Maggie slowly heaves herself out of the car and picks three buttercups to add to the others.

"Come and see, Anita. It's really beautiful."

We drive on and our ears begin to pop. The sun is hot. Orange-tiled roofs and church spires fall away as we climb out of the foothills. The snow-capped Alps float over our heads - up to their icy knees in spring.

We are as high as birds. The air here is sharp and makes us all hungry. Marco finds an auberge and we go in to order sandwiches. Mine is garlic salami. I remember to chew each mouthful 40 times. Then I finish Maggie's.

We drive on through woods of pine, crabbed with lichen on footstools of rock, soft with moss and needles. Marco finds a back-road down the mountain, and we wind our way back, stopping once at the side of the road to gaze at a drift of forget-me-nots. Blue as smoke, they fade into the distance, under the boles of trees. Larks sing overhead. Lower down, we emerge from the wood onto bare hills covered in white rocks and boulders. A farm has arranged some of them into walls that divide the hill into meadows where cows sit down to chew cud and the sheep, time-suspended, lie with their necks stretched out along the ground.

"My God, they all look stoned!"

*

Later on in the afternoon, I go to call home again. This time I get through.

"Mummy, mummy, when are you coming home?"

"I've got a new football."

My children sound so English. Andy takes the phone.

"I've heard of this place in Germany. They do a combination of mild chemotherapy coupled with vitamin therapy and diet."

He is trying to help. I am silent. I don't have words for the reality any more.

"Maggie doesn't stand a chance if she doesn't go the non-traditional route."

Now I just want to scream at him. I hear my voice get cold and sharp. I long to disengage – say goodbye to them all.

"When are you coming home?"

"Soon."

"Goodbye Mummy, I love you."

*

Marco drives me back.

"The hospital here think she' finished. They are givin' her treatment because it is all they know how to do."

"I know. It is easy to forget how, with a terminally ill patient - you are simply on your own."

"Is true."

*

Maggie is terminal. But she isn't terminal all the time. Her death comes as tearful minutes, painful hours, or bad days. Her life is all in between, vital and full of hope. Gradually, I suppose, the balance will drop in favor of her death. But how impossible to believe that we cannot cheat more time from the encroaching shadow - just another afternoon's drive or a moment for a gelatti.

*

My cold has developed into a chest infection.

Yesterday we all got up early and drove to Mestre to search for some rice cakes for Maggie. They don't stock them at the health food shop here. She is obsessive about these rice cakes - sure that they are the only thing she will be able to eat.

It is a long drive, muggy and quiet. I sit in the back, too hot and saying little, Beatles music on the cassette player.

...She's got a ticket to ride, she's got a ticket to ri-i-i-de, she's got a ticket to ride, and she don't care.

We drop in at Oriago, the hamlet where they live. As our car wheels crunch on the gravel, Viola and Maria, Marco's mother, come out of the house.   Over-joyed to see Maggie Maria hugs and kisses her with tears in her eyes.

Then her feelings overflow onto me, and she hugs and kisses me as if somehow, I am responsible for something good. But we can't stay. Maggie is champing to get to Mestre before the shops shut for lunch.

It is a long and fruitless journey, since the two health-food shops don't stock rice cakes. First, Maggie is angry. Then she falls into despair and weeps standing in the gutter of a busy main street, holding onto the car door for support, tears dripping off her nose.

*

We go back to Oriago for lunch. This time, Daisy and Chloe spill out of the house, with Mateo and Maria behind them.

"Mamma! Mamma!"

It is all too much for me. I feel ill and hot and know I am about to cry. I help Maggie inside onto a couch and leave her to her family.

"I'm just off for some fresh air."

"Si, Anita, we come and get you when lunch is ready."

I walk up the garden past a blackbird whistling in a cage, and neat plots of beans and lettuce. I lie down on a bench screened by trees, and fight for control. I can't cry here. I am not alone, and everyone else, except Maggie, is happy. After a while Mateo comes to get me.

"Time to eat, eh Anita."

As we walk back he picks seeds and small leaves from my hair.

"I'm afraid I'm a bit of a mess."

"Yes, you look terrible." He smiles at me.

I am not hungry. Maria points to my plate and says something.

In an Italian household, not eating is a talking point.

"I'm sorry; I'm feeling a bit fluey."

Mateo eats some of my food and hides my unfinished plate from Maria's eagle eye. They are all having some kind of argument that I don't understand.

Mateo explains. "Daisy and Chloe, they go to a birthday party. We take them."

"What about Maggie?"

"She come along too. She can see her friend Diah."

I am very uneasy about this. "Maggie are you going to be okay? You know how you poop out."

But she is stubborn: "No, I feel fine."

We drive to a house full of little girls in party dresses. Everyone is delighted to see Maggie. She limps around the living room talking to Diah, who is giving the party. Marco sits down with a beer and talks with Luca an old friend. I have some coffee and begin to brighten up a bit.

Then Maggie remembers. "Marco, we must get back. Rosie is coming over this evening."

"Porco Dio!"

We have only been there half an hour. Chloe and Daisy wail with outraged eyes, their mouths wide open. We manage to extricate ourselves and leave with the little girls, who are in floods of tears. Marco looks grim. In the car, Maggie tries to explain but they won't listen.

When we get back, they jump out of the car and run up the garden. Maggie see-saws after them. When she comes back with them, they look happy again. She has promised to give them a hamster.

When Maggie gets back into the car, and Marco begins to drive away, Daisy won't let go of the passenger door handle.

Marco and Maggie have a row on the way back to Pordenone.

"Your friend - she could have given them a lift back!"

Maggie argues back in Italian. "The afternoon was mishandled," she says, finally, in English.

"Diah, she never do anything for anybody. She's a bitch."

Maggie defends her in Italian.

Back at Pordenone, Rosie doesn't show up. Maggie gets into bed and we play cards until bed-time.

*

Today, Marco left early again.

"I don't want her to 'ave any more chemotherapy."

In the afternoon I try to prepare Maggie for Marco's return. We are in the kitchen, and I am washing up.

"Are you sure you want to go back to hospital?"

"I don't know."

"The thing is, if you have any doubts, now is the time to think it through - while you are clear headed and cheerful. When the chemotherapy starts, you'll be too ill."

I speak gently, conscious that I cause her pain when I ask her to think ahead.

"I wish I could be sure that natural diet and vitamins would work."

"You can't be sure about that. But you can't be sure of the chemotherapy either."

"I wish I knew how many of these treatments I could have."

"Well, perhaps you could go and see your own doctor in the hospital and ask him. Use this time to find out what you can, so that you can make some decisions."

She closes her eyes and leans her head against the wall. "When it comes to making decisions, it's like night coming on."

"So don't make a decision. Just use this time to find out what you can. Take it one step at a time."

She is silent. I can see she has clammed up.

As gently as I can: "As far as the hospital is concerned, Maggie, the outcome must look very doubtful."

There is a long silence. Then she says firmly. "I have to have a doctor to go to, Anita. I'm very conservative."

"That's understandable. They have had some success. They have shrunk the tumor, and you have much less pain."

"Yes. That's true."

*

Last Christmas she was in such pain with "sciatica'" that she was prescribed morphine.

"I finally went to an osteopath and he took one look at my bottom and said: *Signora, go to hospital and get an X-ray.* "

Maggie's eyes get vicious.

"When the doctor came down from the X-ray department I could see that he was pleased. *You have cancer* he said. I could see it in his eyes, he was a sadist. They took me straight in and gave me the cobalt."

*

Later, we go outside for a short walk, in the public space between the apartment blocks. We find a bench in the shade of a willow, and sit side by side, with the long grass pushing up around our legs and through the slats. The willow leans low and sighs over our heads.

"I remember looking out of my bedroom window and wondering what the fuck I was doing here. I was so bored."

"How old were you?"

"I don't know. Very young. I must have been about four years old."

*

When Marco comes home, he tells me that Mateo is going to Switzerland. He has hunted down some Laetrile for Maggie. The alternative treatment of vitamin B17 extracted from apricot seeds. He will go on Sunday, his day off.

*

A bad day and I sleep all of it. I am feverish. Maggie's hair falls out in handfuls. She goes out with Marco to buy scarves. As they leave without me I hear her say:

"I hope Anita is all right."

*

When night falls, I get up. Maggie is restless, unable to settle. They are out of yogurt, and, as tomorrow is Sunday, she cannot have any until Monday. As with the rice cakes she is certain that it is the one thing that she will be able to eat.

"There is nothing for me to eat. What shall I eat? I have to eat."

"If Mateo is going to Switzerland tomorrow, perhaps he could pick up some from Oriago. He plans to come here in any case."

"Okay, Anita." Marco goes out to the public phone box - a harassed figure with jingling keys.

But when he comes back events have changed.

"Mateo does not go to Switzerland. He has found another doctor in Italy. He does natural therapy. He can get the B17 from this Doctor."

Maggie says nothing. She is impatient - focused on yogurt.

"I go myself to Oriago an' get the yogurt."

"No. It's too far to go," Maggie insists.
"Surely you could go tomorrow," I conciliate.

Marco is adamant. They argue and in the end Maggie insists on going with him. I decide to go too.

*

We prop Maggie in the passenger seat with pillows, hot water bottle, and a rug. We take off to the Beatles 60's hits. The night is fresh and it is good to be on the move. It starts to rain heavily, and we drive into our headlights needled with black arrows. Maggie relaxes in the moving car and Marco holds her hand all the way.

And when I touch you I feel happy inside. It's such a feeling, that my love, I can't hide.

When we arrive, everyone is up except the little girls who are upstairs asleep. Maria, Viola and Mateo crowd around Maggie talking Italian, but she is restless and weepy.

She won't sit down and wants to be off again. They insist that she go upstairs to see the children, and bunch her upstairs. I want to stay behind, but Maria, the last of the family group, urges me up with her arm.

In the children's room, rain patters on the roof. They are sprawled asleep, with their hair spread and their toys arranged around them. Maggie stays for only a moment and then goes back downstairs, eager to be gone.

I am left with Mateo. He sits at the foot of Daisy's bed his hands joined together, elbows on knees. He looks straight ahead. I whisper:

"It's good news about this new Doctor."

"Si, Anita. I don't know everything yet, but I will speak with him on Monday."

Downstairs, Maggie wants to be gone. She cannot bear to be kept waiting. I hurry down into their argument. Marco has the yogurt as well as other provisions from Maria.

As we begin to back out of the drive Maggie bursts into tears.

"Daisy, Chloe."

Her voice cries out into the rain. Marco stops the car and everyone outside leans into the passenger window to soothe her. They all get wet as the rain falls onto their backs. They promise to bring the children over to Pordenone tomorrow.

I know Maggie does not want to see them tomorrow. She weeps, not because she missed them tonight, but because she can do nothing for them anymore, and must leave their care to Maria and Viola. She feels separated from them by an ever-widening gap.

I feel terrible. Perhaps I have shocked her. She is so delicately balanced. So far, she has managed to keep most of this at bay by leaving everything to everyone else. She asks me no questions and even when she does I cannot speak the truth. I have done nothing but interfere with her chosen way of coping with all of this.

*

Maggie is very restless after another bad night. She is in pain. I give her a massage which soothes her only a little. The base of her spine is lumpy. Some of the lumps are attached, hard little stones of tension, but some float free, as nodules of soft fat. I move my fingers in small circles on her spine and on either side of it, over her pelvis.

She cannot stay still. She moves from the bedroom to the kitchen, from the living room, back to her bedroom. She cannot get comfortable anywhere.

It is as if her body has a life of its own and has turned into a wild animal that longs to break free of its cage. Endlessly, it turns and paces, looks for a chink or a carelessly turned key – like the Grey Crow in the park, incessantly hopping back and forth, from one perch to another, all its inability to fly away reduced to this one obsessive action.

I stroke her, sit with her, talk and keep silent, but it makes no difference.

The children are due, and she puts on makeup and a bright yellow bandana. You can see her scalp clearly now. It shines through at the back of her head, where it lies on the pillows, and at her temples, where it has receded.

At four o'clock, they still haven't come. Marco goes out to phone.

"They have just left," he says, when he gets back.

Maggie is furious. "Why didn't they stay? It's too late."

"They fell asleep."

*

We drive her into the fields again, in an attempt to soothe her, and she does finally calm down. She sits, quiet at last with the window open, her thin, bandanaed profile silhouetted against the mountains. Over our heads they are clear after the rain. Unshakable, they rise up, over the skyline. Like the sea, the mountains will still be here when we are all gone.

"I can only relax in the country."

We watch two children come home to their farm. They get off a country bus and, as they walk towards the farmhouse, two horses loose in their box, cavort their welcome.

Joyous neighing rings out over the fields.

*

When we go home, Daisy and Chloe have just arrived with Mateo and Viola. The kids are tired and scratchy after their long journey. Mateo suggests ice cream.

"You come too, eh, Anita."

"Yes, I can show you the way." I guide them into Pordenone. At last something I can do. I long to get away from Maggie and her restlessness.

After Daisy and Chloe finish their ice cream, they go off and play. Over a cappuccino, I talk to Viola, with Mateo as translator. I ask her how the children are taking it. Have they asked any questions?

Daisy has asked if Maggie is dying.

"She say that if her mama is dying she is sure she will go to heaven, because she has suffered so much. The nuns say that all those who suffer go to heaven."

Chloe has not asked anything.

*

Maggie woke up this morning eager for the day, confident that she slept well. I feel better myself and, spirits up, we chatter on her bed. Marco teases her.

"Last night I put a suppository up your arse, and you didn't even wake up. You were very restless and moaning. You were so asleep that you didn't even notice."

"Charmed, I'm sure."

"I could have fucked you, and you wouldn't have known."

Maggie laughs.

"Don't think it has escaped my notice that you are giving me the date rape drug."

But, when we go for another drive - to capitalize on her high spirits, she gets more and more restless. She cannot get comfortable on the seat. She moves from buttock to buttock, wincing in pain. Back home, she returns to bed and cannot eat.

She lies on her back, with her legs curled over onto her belly and holds onto her knees with her hands. In this fetal position, she finds relief, as all her weight is on her upper back. "Anita," she calls, "come here."

I move over to her and she pulls an ivory and turquoise ring off her hand. I have admired it several times. "I want you to have this."

I don't know what to say. Passionately, I don't want it. Not only because Marco gave it to her, but because I don't want her to give me anything. It is too much like the settling of effects.

My hands are smaller than hers, and I put it on the same finger she took it off from. It is too big. As it is ivory, not metal, it cannot be made to fit.

"Thank you Maggie, but I am afraid it is too big. I will lose it."

"Put it on your middle finger." Maggie, ever practical, sees the solution. I do, and it fits perfectly.

"But, Marco gave it to you. He might be offended."

"I want you to have it."

As soon as I can, I go into the kitchen, and show it to Marco who is washing up.

"Look, Maggie gave me this." I hold out my hand.

He says nothing but smiles and kisses me gently. I realize that they have arranged this together. They both want me to have it.

*

By evening, Maggie is in pain. She is restless and fearful. She cannot eat and is afraid that she will lose the little ground she has gained. It is obvious that she will not be able to sleep. I ask Marco to call in the doctor again. Perhaps he can prescribe a painkiller, or a potent sleeping pill.

When he comes, he stands over her bed and listens gravely. Her voice complains and whines as she confides in him. I know she is going on and on about not being able to eat - and more weakness.

"No mangiare più," she says. "I don't eat anymore."

Her face is earnest, like a little girl who explains why she cannot do as she is told. His face is serious and he nods often. He gives her a shot of vitamins and leaves a Rohypnol, a sleeping pill that she already has.

I do not understand these doctors at all. Maggie has a painful terminal disease. I cannot believe that there is not an adequate pain-killer that she can have, so that she can enjoy the life left to her.

He goes into the kitchen with Marco to consult. After he has gone, I join Marco next to the washing up.

"He give her three months at the most. He say that she is very bad."

"How does he know?" I am indignant and protective.

"Because he say her face is green. The cancer is all through her."

"Well, I don't think that's a very professional basis for an opinion. "Anyway, her face isn't green."

'They all pricks', agrees Marco.

*

Maggie takes the pill, and dozes off. Marco and I go into the kitchen and play an Italian board game, a bit like checkers, on the kitchen table. He pulls out the Grappa and we get drunk. Marco talks of love and we argue like grave diggers. In a kind of drunken brilliance, I beat him hands down at the game.

"Fuckin' shit," he keeps saying, as I sweep the board clean of his pieces yet again. "I jus'don' understand it."

Maggie comes in. She is cross and wants Marco to come to bed.

"Would you like me to stay with her?" I ask, sober now.

"No, Anita, you get some sleep."

But it is impossible to sleep. Maggie moans in the other room, and my bed spins round and round. I get up at 3:30 for a drink of water and meet Marco in the hall. I offer again to stay with her, but again he refuses. Maggie paces about, bleary-eyed and wild.

*

Maggie and Marco are pasty and exhausted. They haven't slept all night. Marco is furious. He goes out for food. Maggie weeps with exhaustion and fear. Her back is very painful. When Marco returns, they fight. He is at the end of his tether. He hasn't slept for three nights. He's wasted.

"What do you want me to do? I can do nothing for you. Nothing." He waves his hands about and chops at the air.

"Marco, why don't we take her to the hospital to ask them for some decent pain-killers, and get some more adequate sleeping pills. They must be able to help her."

Maggie nods through her tears and Marco goes storming out again to phone the hospital.

Very slowly I help her put her clothes on. I comb her hair and it comes out in handfuls. She is almost completely bald at the back, and, from behind, her head is a baby's head.

Marco comes back. "You go into 'ospital now. They take you today. You go in in two days anyway." He spits it out.

Maggie wails. "No! No! No voglio. I just want an injection, no?"

Marco yells and shouts in Italian. He goes out onto the kitchen balcony. Maggie sobs. I follow him out into the bright morning snipped with swallows.

"Marco." I put my arms around him. "Let's just get them to give her an injection and see what happens. It is at least worth a try. If it doesn't work, it doesn't work. She wants to stay here and it's good for her."

He immediately softens and goes back in to comfort and apologize to Maggie.

"We get you an injection Maggie. You see. Don't worry."

Marco is remarkable. The smallest demand on his good will, the smallest affectionate gesture, and he is back into battle, his exhaustion put aside.

*

At the hospital, we go straight to the nurses' station where they talk to her in soft voices. Sympathetic and serious they listen to her tale of woe and mounting pain. A doctor appears and asks that she be put to bed. We slowly limp down the hall into a room with two beds - undress her and put her to bed.

An old woman with grey stubble on her head lies in the other bed, covered by a single, white sheet.

Her feet stick out at the bottom. She looks straight ahead, her arms folded over her head and her mouth set in a grim line. Beside her sits another, younger woman, who speaks occasionally. The old woman's only reply is a grunt.

After we are settled, the younger woman takes the olds woman's legs, one at a time, and gently pumps them over her stomach. We look away, so as not to see the grey fur between her legs. Then the younger woman insists that the old woman also exercise her arms. With no word, no alteration of the grim, set expression, the old woman clasps her hands over her head, and moves her arms from side to side. Then the two of them lapse into silence. They both look like ships in a storm, hatches battened down, sails trimmed to a minimum.

I start to cry and go into the bathroom. There is no toilet paper so I dry my eyes on my T-shirt.

When the doctor comes in, he prods Maggie, and agrees to give her an injection of pure aspirin - injected into the site of the pain. Soon after, a young nurse bustles in with a kidney bowl, a filled syringe, cotton wool and alcohol. She sits behind Maggie and gets her to curl into a ball. Then she administers the shot next to Maggie's spine. Maggie bursts into tears and writhes about on the bed. I hold her in my arms and rub the spot where the needle went in.

The nurse is bewildered by Maggie's reaction. She tells Marco that it shouldn't hurt like that. After a while the pain subsides and Maggie lies back, more comfortable now. I stroke the top of her head with my fingertips, and silent, we watch the old woman, who has started her exercises again.

*

Later on, to everyone's surprise, Mateo walks in.

We had all forgotten he promised to take me shopping in Venice to buy some souvenirs for my children and a birthday present for Andy.

When he found that we weren't at the flat, he guesses where we are and comes to get me. I refuse to leave, but Maggie and Marco insist.

"You go, Anita, have a good time."

"We be here for a long time. I be with Maggie. Go."

I vacillate, confused and tearful, but Mateo grabs me by the arm and pulls me from the room. Marco escorts us to the lift. The doors close on his smiling face.

*

Mateo's car is battered and the passenger seat is so collapsed, that I have to lean back with my legs up on the dash board. We drive through green cornfields, brilliant with poppies. The wind blows on my face through the open window.

When we arrive in Venice we park and walk into the main vaporetto terminal, to catch a water bus.

"Jus' do me one favor. Please don' buy a gondolier's hat." They are for sale hung in bunches near the gang planks - cheap undersized imitations of the real things. "If you do, I don' walk with you."

I laugh and promise not to.

"Where do you wan' go?"

"What I'd really like is to get lost. Just get on a boat, and end up anywhere."

"You joking!"

"No. I'm perfectly serious."

"Okay, Anita. I try."

We walk up a gang plank with all the other tourists. It is cool near the water with its wet smacking sounds under the hull. The vaporetto takes us round the corner to the bus station and stops.

"If you really want to see Venice, you mus' go with a Venetian."

"Well I must say, viewing the bus station isn't quite what I had in mind."

We get onto another boat, and sit in the stern, outside, in the sunshine. A flag blows in my face until the boat moves off. Then we chug into Venice and fold into the canals, between the faded terracotta, saffron, green, gold and pink of Venetian palaces.

The paint looks as if it was applied three hundred years ago and the lower stories are slapped by floating rubbish and bobbing boats. Steps disappear into the jade water and doors and windows are sunk into their own weaving reflections. Swallows skim and twinkle everywhere.

I want to see the blue and gold clock tower with the winged lion, so we get off the boat at Piazza San Marco. Mateo tells me about an American girl he met, one summer, when he worked in the square as a waiter.

"She want me to screw her right in the middle of St Marco."

"Good heavens. How public!"

"I know. But she insist."

"Do you suppose she came abroad to be ravished on all the major European monuments?"

"Maybe".

*

Mateo gets us lost, and the day winds away as we walk through narrow flag-stoned streets, past squares, with plashing fountains, lazy with cats. We catch glimpses of dappled green gardens, shady and secret.

Occasionally we stop for cappuccino and later for wine. Flowers are everywhere -window-boxes of geranium and roses. Weeds push through the flagstones, and hobbling, coral-toed pigeons bow and turn.

We pause by a narrow canal under an arch. I sit on the steps in the damp shade, chin on my knees, and watch white, fluffy seeds as they float down onto the water. We are near a bridge, and I stare at the wriggling reflection of its wrought-iron balustrade, caught in some invisible current. Mateo is quiet and smokes a cigarette, until my numb bottom indicates it is time to move on, back into the sun again.

When dusk falls, it is time to leave. Under a full moon and Venus, the first star, Mateo and I have a cross-purpose conversation:

He is indignant because I mention Christians thrown to the lions. This has touched a patriotic nerve.

"The Colosseum in Rome was built for sheep."

"What?"

"It was built for sheep. They flood it with water for the sheep. And then they make battles."

"Sheep?"

"Yes, sheep."

I realize he must means 'ships,' not sheep, and laugh so hard I have to hold onto some balustrades.

Mateo is mystified. "Wha' is so funny?"

"Christian martyrs swimming around in a sheep dip."

"Wha' you talkin' about?"

*

When we get back to Pordenone, Maggie is comfortable at last, but very drugged. I sit next to her and she talks of Daisy and Chloe.

"I wish they had grown up English."

Marco and Mateo are obviously insulted, but, oblivious of their reaction, Maggie rambles on.

"The English are so eccentric. They may look very conservative on the outside, but inside, they're all eccentrics."

I realize that she is as high as a kite. But the brothers argue with her, their sad, gingery faces reflect one another in the shadows around her bed.

"Everyone is the same," they say.

"No, no. The English are different. Anita knows what I mean."

She takes hold of my hand. "Anita opened my mind," she says, drowsy.

I am dumbfounded.

Alone in my room, while everyone sleeps, I burst into tears. They are the kind of tears that feed upon themselves and don't run dry, so I get up and go onto the kitchen balcony to smoke a cigarette. In the cold, I shiver looking down into the yellow streetlights and the dead, sloping shadow of a cat.

If I opened Maggie's mind, it was she who opened my heart.

*

Maggie is awake, dapper and confident, her pain under control. She slept well. I brush her hair and scads of it come out. I pluck it from her hair brush and put it down behind her on the bed where she won't see. Marco picks it up, hides it behind his back and leaves the bedroom. I hear the toilet flush.

She gets dressed in a royal blue track suit with a yellow and red cotton bandana. Bright as a butterfly, she limps downstairs, and we all get into the car with a picnic Marco has prepared. We speed along in the sunshine with Ry Cooder on the tape.

Baby I'll give you the clothes off my back
I'll give you everything I've got in my shack
But if you ever try to leave me, they'll take you out in a sack
Me and my razor will see to that.

"They are tha' way in the South here too."

*

We drive back up into the mountains. At midday, we pull off the road to eat our picnic. Maggie questions what Marco put in the sandwiches.

"What have you put in here? Is there any cheese? You forgot the knife."

Marco gets out to stretch his legs, and disappears into the trees. Maggie talks about her English friends.

Maggie belongs to a women's group, made up of English-speaking women whose only common ground is that they married Italian men. They are a hybrid community, ranging in age from 18 to 52, and include English, Australian, American, Jamaican, and Javanese Diah who wouldn't give Chloe and Daisy a lift back from her party.

"We get together to bitch about our Italian husbands."

When Maggie was in hospital, they all visited her and ganged up on Marco about her treatment. They believe that her only chance is to stay in hospital, and don't understand Marco's insistence that she stay at home.

The tension upset Maggie and she is afraid that her friends have deserted her. The truth is everyone is still in shock.

Suddenly, I remember that I am due to go back home today. Maggie's illness has overtaken all my other commitments. I can't bear to leave her when she is suffering, and I can't bear to leave her when she is feeling better. I find Marco, smoking under a tree.

"Marco, I must call Andy. They are expecting me back today."

"Fuckin' shit!."

We dash into Pordenone, drop Maggie off, and at the Telefono Pubblico, I get through.

"But we have spring cleaned the house."

"'We got you a Mother's Day present."

"When are you coming home?"

My children's voices are disappointed and tearful. I promise them I'll come home Friday.

I pay the cashier, very quiet. Marco grabs my arm and marches me off for a cappuccino.

"You must go back. They need you."

"But I want to stay'."

"I know. But you can't. You must go home."

I know he wants me to stay because when I go he is all alone with Maggie's death. Marco is very bitter about last night and Maggie's rejection of all things Italian. Soon he is raving over his cappuccino.

"She never wan' to make love wi me. Never. I don' understand it. I know she enjoy it, but she never want to do it. Once, I left her alone for four months, I waited for her to want to, but she never do anything. I couldn't stand it. I couldn't wait anymore. I couldn't stand it. I tell her she can go home, she don't have to stay with me."

I am embarrassed. I am sure Maggie doesn't want me to know the details of her married life. We never spoke of sex.

"She never tell me about John her first boyfriend. I know she still hate him, after all these years. I don' understand this. Why does she still hate him? She never talk about herself. She never talk about anything. I can't stand it."

"Marco, you must understand. Maggie is English. We are brought up to ignore sex, to think of it as dangerous and bad. Her parents didn't care about her - show her any affection...."

But Marco is past sympathy. He raves on and on. He is suspicious of her and of what he thinks she is hiding. I shut up and smoke.

*

Back at the flat, I finish my packing, and we all sit around the kitchen table for some Grappa.

To my horror, Marco gets drunk and goes for Maggie, yelling in Italian, and bits of English.

I know he feels her entry into hospital tomorrow is her final rejection of him, and what he can do for her. But he attacks her for her sexual coldness.

She is silent. She nods occasionally at his accusations with a set face. I can't bear it. Desperate to sober up - I interfere.

"Maggie, is there anything about Marco that pleases you?"

"Oh yes." Her smile is tender. "I like the way he touches me."

Marco, of course, hasn't heard a word. Incensed and drunk, he carries on.

"Marco, you are not listening. Did you hear what she just said?"

"Wha'? She don' say nothing."

"Yes. She did. She said she likes the way you touch her. Say it again Maggie."

"I like the way you touch me." Again, her smile is soft.

Marco looks surprised.

"The trouble is, you don't listen," I say.

"Yes, that's true. But she don' tell me nothing."

"Well what do you want to know? You make a lot of statements, but you ask no questions."

"Tell me abou' John."

"He fucked me."

"Great." I interrupt the silence. "'I think we need a little more detail: Where?"

"It was in his flat."

"Why did you fuck him?"

"Because he wanted to, and I was in love with him."

'What was it like?'

"Christ!" says Marco. "You morbid."

"Yes, I always want to know the details."

"Anita knows how to ask the right questions."

"So what was it like?"

"I just lay there. I didn't feel a thing. Are you sure you want to do this? he said. Afterwards, he told me to knock on the door when I came to see him, in case he was with someone else."

"Was he screwing other girls then?"

"Yes. He ended up marrying one of them. It was because she was rich. He liked me I know. But he went with her because she had money. I cried so hard that my false eyelashes curled right back into my eyelids."

"So you continued with him, sharing his favors so to speak, until he went steady with a rich girl."

"Yes."

*

The swinging sixties. Maggie, her hair cut into a Mary Quant - skinny with tight, thigh-length dresses and long, false eyelashes alone in London, is working as a waitress in a fashionable restaurant. I am in Oxford working in Woolworths, to support my sculpture class at the local Polytechnic.

Maggie doesn't want to live in Oxford. She prefers London where it is all happening. Sex, drugs and rock and roll. I made no secret that I thought Maggie's taste in men was ghastly.

Down in London from Oxford, I stand on her doorstep, while she looks for her key.

By coincidence, John the de-flowerer comes down the street to take out Maggie's rich flat-mate from New Zealand. I know he has hurt Maggie.

She looks at my face as we watch him come up the steps and hisses:

Anita, please don't say anything. Don't say anything.

So I contain myself when he turns on the charm. *So this is the famous Anita.*

John is exactly the kind of lost, self-serving soul I would have crossed the street to avoid.

*

"I didn't tell you Anita, because I felt that I had let you down."

"You didn't let me down Maggie. Anyway, I wasn't a virgin anymore, either, and my story is just as sad as yours."

"I tell you my first time." Marco reaches for the Grappa.

"She was from Newcastle, on holiday. I know we wan' one another and I know where she has her room in the hotel, where I am a waiter. I have to climb up three floors on the outside, so no one see me. When I am with her I take my time with her, and we make love. We both enjoy it and we are lovers until she leaves. When she go, I bring her flowers. She is getting on the bus, and she cry when she leave."

"Did you see her again?"

"Yes. I go to Newcastle, bu' it doesn' work. It is not the same again."

Maggie and Marco start to argue in Italian. With no phrases in English I know it is my cue to leave them. I am very drunk and stumble on my way to my room. In bed, I hear them talking together for a long time before I drift into a dizzy sleep.

In the early hours of the morning Marco bursts in.

"Wha' happen to the psychiatrist?" he yells. Maggie shushes him in the background.

*

Another brilliant morning.

I wake up with hot coals in the pit of my stomach. My head hurts and I'm tired out. In the car, the sunny atmosphere is baleful, the streets like fly paper. Maggie on her way to hospital feels like Maggie on her way to the abattoir.

They have put her in the same room as before, with the same grizzled and paralyzed old woman. We unpack Maggie's clothes and a few books. She is cheerful and calm. The hospital gives her confidence.

A nurse comes in with a computer card to ask Maggie what she wants to eat for lunch. Maggie explains that the doctors have told her not eat at all, as she is to start chemotherapy. Never-the-less, the nurse has to know. She punches out a computer card with her pen, asking Maggie multiple choice questions about beans or peas, pasta or minestrone.

"Dio Christo!" yells the old woman from the next bed. Her first words.

*

Marco returns and sits down opposite me.

"Well?"

"Well, what?"

"The story of your first fuck. You don't think you get away with it, do you?"

I see that Maggie is listening intently. We have never spoken to one another about our sex lives before.

So I tell her, through Marco.

"His name was Bill - an American GI. I met him when he was on leave in the south of Spain. I liked him a lot.

He was intelligent, humorous and fiery, and irritated by my virginity.

He couldn't understand why, at twenty-three, I still hadn't gone the whole way. I suppose I was annoying. He once said:

Jesus, Anida, if I dropped you out of a helicopter in the middle of the desert, you'd find your way home.

He was kind to me and when he offered me the lift back to London – I was glad to accept.

On the first overnight stop, he booked a double room, and we slept in single, separate beds. The next morning, he was peevish and asked me to get into bed with him. Compelled by a sense of obligation because he paid for the room, I did so. He held me and then tried to climb onto me. I drew back. *Trust me*, he pleads. I do. He climbs onto my prone and frozen body, parts my legs, and calmly enters me for one thrust before he gets off again.

Well, he said, *you're not a virgin anymore.*

"This is no way to fuck a woman."

"Bill didn't want to fuck me - he just wanted my virginity, to be able to say he had been the first."

"This is a really stupid thing to do," says Marco. He slowly shakes his head.

"Perhaps he wanted to be sure I would never forget him. And I won't. It is a kind of immortality, I suppose."

*

It is time to leave. Marco has to drive me to Oriago to change my ticket for the flight home tomorrow.

On the drive, I go for Marco. I want to defend Maggie.

"You don't listen, you know. When you are hurt you build a wall around yourself - a wall of theory and paranoia that you don't check out. You just assume you know, and you don't ask the most ordinary questions.

You simply cannot know you are right. You cut yourself off and throw away your gifts of understanding and wholeness.   You think like a peasant."

We are both very heated by the time we drive up to the house in Oriago.

"Bu' you' exactly the same..." he yells - but our conversation is never finished.

The children run out of the house and Marco gets on the phone about my ticket. I need to be alone and write a note to Marco:

Gone for a walk on the canal.

I hurry over the road, through a farm yard, and up the steep bank. The grass hisses, obscuring the path as I push my way along, plucking at the grass heads as they swim past my hips.

Far from the house, I let myself cry, hands full of seeds.

I just don't know how to say goodbye to you, Maggie, I whisper. *I just don't know how to do it.*

When I return, Marco has gone, but Mateo has just arrived and stands next to his car in the driveway.

"Marco can get your ticket. You go tomorrow at 11am."

Marco has arranged for Mateo to take me from Pordenone to the airport tomorrow.

I am stunned. I expected to stay until Monday. Mateo takes two necklaces out from his glove compartment.

"I get these for you. Perhaps one will be good for Cariad."

I am without words, and reluctant to take them.

"You mustn't worry, Anita," he laughs, misunderstanding. "It cost me very little, believe me."

He fastens a string of tiny red garnets around my neck.

"It suit you."

*

On the long drive back to Pordenone, Mateo side tracks, and drives into the grounds of an old Villa, that once belonged to Italian aristocracy. We wander around the grounds and Mateo talks of Lady Chatterley's Lover

He is aggressive. Our walk becomes tense. I realize I put my foot in it when I accused Marco of thinking like a peasant. To confront one of them is to confront them both.

*

It is night when we return to the flat at Pordenone. Marco is waiting for us with the news that Maggie started chemotherapy earlier today. She has already vomited twice and is upset that I have to leave early tomorrow.

*

Marco left early on an errand, and it is Mateo who drives me across town to say goodbye to Maggie.

At the hospital, we get into the lift together along with a man in pajamas. Mateo strikes up a conversation and they both double up with laughter. When we get off on the seventh floor, the lift doors closes on the man still doubled over slapping his knee.

"What on earth were you talking about?"

"He tell me that whenever he get into a lift, he is afraid there will be an earthquake. I say that if that happen the lift will be full of shit. Then he say that whenever he get into a lift he always want to shit."

We walk up the long shiny corridor into Maggie's room. As soon as I walk in I smell vomit. Maggie is asleep. When I touch her she is hot. She wakes up, grumpy.

"Madonna, that woman snored so loud I couldn't sleep." She glares at the old woman in the next bed. "Porco Dio!" she shouts.

The old woman, with her grey stubble, laughs. Her mouth is a black hole with no teeth.

Tactful, Mateo leaves. I am here to say goodbye. I lie back on the bed and wonder when I will cry again. Maggie whitters on.

"The doctors won't let me eat anything. I'm sure I should be having something."

A nurse trundles in with a weighing machine.

Maggie heaves herself out of bed and steps onto the scales. She tells the nurse in Italian that she wants to eat something. The nurse nods and slides the weights up the scale. Maggie has lost two pounds since yesterday.

I feel myself go dead. There is no more fear of tears. Somehow, the metal weighing machine has cut me off from myself.

Marco and Mateo come in together along with another nurse who has breakfast for the old woman.

The old woman is paralyzed and Mateo helps her to drink caffè latte from a bowl. She sucks at the straw, her head turned sideways on the pillow. Without teeth, she cannot help dribbling, and he wipes her lips. I look on with all the connection of a shucked insect skin.

It is time to go. I lean over Maggie and hold her for a moment.

"Goodbye Maggie. I must go now and catch my plane."

"Goodbye. Thanks for coming." She does not look at me, but over my shoulder.

"I'll come back when you're out of here. I'll be here to look after you again."

"What about Andy. Won't he mind?" She meets my eyes.

"No, he'll be all right. He isn't working right now. I'm going back for the children."

"You must go. You'll miss your plane."

"Goodbye." I hug her again, and leave, turning only at the door.

"See you."

"Tara." Our old way of saying goodbye.

"Tara"

Marco has disappeared again and downstairs Mateo ushers me into his car.

"Where's Marco?' I haven't said goodbye."

"He's coming too."

"But why two cars?" I fret.

"Wait, Anita."

We drive down the turnpike. Tired and hung over, I try to doze. Against my eyelids I see thousands of scarlet poppies. At the toll exit for Oriago, we pull over and stop.

"Why have we stopped?"

"Wait, Anita."

In a short while, Marco drives up. He gets out of his car with a bunch of orchids, for me. He hugs me.

"Goodbye, Anita. Thank you for coming." His touch is warm and brisk. "I must go now. Goodbye. Have a good trip."

I realize that he doesn't think I'm coming back. He gets back into his car, U-turns in front of the toll gates, waves, and speeds off.

*

On the drive with Mateo to the airport, I tell him about my first meeting with Marco at the Royal Festival Hall.

"I was very suspicious of him because I thought he was one of Maggie's sharks. But, when I saw him, I knew immediately that he was a good man.

I think you are both very nice men. You are both very reassuring. Somehow everything is better when you are around."

"Marco and me we think you look very English. When you walk, your nose go in the air, so." He points skyward.

"And you walk with your back very straight."

I laugh at this image of myself.

"Men notice you. When you walk into a bar they all know you are there. Bu', you know this very well."

"Yes, but I don't like it."

"Yes, you do. You wouldn't like it if we didn't notice you."

Then he laughs.

I'm angry. Now I dislike him intensely.

If this is flirtation it is not going very well.

*

Marco has booked my flight from a military airport. The noise is astounding. Jets take off and land at regular intervals. Their screams preclude conversation, so, Mateo and I don't say much, but watch the military come and go - as well as their families who arrange their luggage and their children, ready for the civilian flight to London.

When it is time to go, I walk into passport control and out onto the tarmac. Mateo blows me a kiss from behind a wire fence.

June

This time it is Mateo who meets me at the airport. He takes my luggage and pilots me by the elbow into the car park - brings me up to date.

"We find a new treatment for her. I go to a convention with many, many doctors, and I find this doctor who does heat treatments. Her last chemotherapy treatment was so bad she couldn't finish. So now we find something else."

"How does it work?"

"They put heat on the cancer and sometime it make it smaller."

"Where is Maggie now?"

"She go to Zingonia yesterday with Marco and Viola. That is where the doctor does his work. They start her new treatment soon."

"Where will I be staying?"

"Marco and Viola rent some rooms in Zingonia. You will stay with them near the 'ospital. You go the day . . . after . . . tomorrow. Yes? That is right?"

"If you mean Wednesday. Yes. The day after tomorrow."

"The day after tomorrow." Mateo nods and leans back into his seat as he negotiates a corner - the fields turning around his profile.

*

Mateo must do some shopping for Maria. In a grocery store the owners offer us some slices of cheese. Their son goes into the back, for a bottle of red wine, clicking through a bead curtain. Over our glasses, the wife asks after Maggie. I know because her eyes fill with tears. Mateo is grave. Then he turns to me and asks me what I think of the wine.

I reply without thinking. "It's a bit fruity."

Mateo bursts out laughing, and bends in half to slap his knee. They all smile at me.

"Eh, Anita, we can't give you English any old shit."

*

Mateo takes me and the girls to the beach. With Daisy and Chloe, we sit on the sand, who build sand castles, decorating them with odd bits of shell and weed. We talk of astrology.

"I have Leo rising, too. I'm afraid it means we both have a need to be liked."

"Si. This is true. I hate it if people don' like me an' I try everything to make them like me."

Then he takes us all to an open-air seafood restaurant, on a river, to enjoy an Italian fry-up of octopus and fish, and dry white wine. I look out over the cool water, as it refracts the scattered sky and watch the swallows skim the surface for insects. Stray cats beg for scraps, and then crouch growling at one another.

"If I was a Leo, I would say, "I love you," remarks Mateo.

*

Mateo touches my hair at 4:30 am. I wake with a start and then turn into my pillow longing for more time. He shakes my shoulder until I am properly awake.

"Anita, we must go soon."

Outside it is raining hard, with rumbles of thunder and flashes of lightning. I dress quickly, gather my luggage and go downstairs into the groaning dark.

We pack up the car in waves of perfume released from the rain-drenched flowers, and drive off into a dawning day, the windscreen wipers working overtime to wipe away streams of water as our headlights pick out the road ahead. We don't speak. As we speed towards Maggie, my senses stretch ahead, trying to intuit her frame of mind.

In Zingonia, we come upon Marco and Viola walking down the street deep in conversation. Mateo skids up beside them. Viola jumps and then laughs when she sees who it is. She looks very tired and says something to me.

Marco and Mateo translate. "Maggie don' want her. She only want you."

"For Viola there is no difference between Italian people and English people."

Viola nods her face grave. Marco is angry again.

"She won' fight. She have another nervous breakdown, when she find out what this new treatment cost. It is only natural, no? We do the same for anyone in the family."

"How much does it cost?"

"Is not important. I don't understand her. She is scared to owe money. It is only natural we do what we can for her."

Again, nothing Marco does for her brings relief.

"I am sorry, Anita. You have to stay with Maggie, and we take Viola home. She only want you, she don't want us."

If she stay she only inhibit you an Maggie."

"Really, it's okay. I came to be with Maggie. It's okay.

Marco has rented a pensione on a busy main road, down the road from the hospital. They show me into a room with two single beds. Through the window, I watch them get into the car. Small though they are, I can see from their movements how relieved they are to be off. They have all had more than enough of Maggie.

My walk to the hospital is down a featureless main road with lorries swooping past. Their drivers blat their horns and call out in Italian. I am glad when a stray dog follows me, bouncing in and out of the undergrowth after lizards.

*

The lift doors open onto the smell of ether and my breath stops for a moment. Marco has told me Maggie's room is right at the end of the corridor, the farthest away from the nurses' station. When I open the door, she is in bed with a bright red scarf wrapped around her head. A doctor and nurse are examining a patient in the next bed and wave me out of the room. Maggie grins and I duck back out.

When they leave, serious faced, in their white overalls, I go back in and hug Maggie.

"Viola seems to think you are fed up with her."

"It's true. Viola makes me tired. She talks so much. She thinks very hard about everything and gives me too much to think about."

*

To begin with, Maggie is in good spirits and we chatter together about nothing in particular, stared at by the woman in the next bed. By lunch time her mood changes.

"I cannot eat. I am afraid my stomach will close up if I don't, but I cannot eat it.'"

The nurse puts her lunch on the table for her, and urges her: "Mangiare, mangiare."

Maggie limps over, but her bottom makes the briefest contact with the chair, before she is up again, and swaying back to bed.

She begins to cry. "I feel so bad about owing so much money."

"Don't you feel you are worth it?"

"No, I don't." She curls up on the bed and closes her eyes.

I go and eat her lunch.

After a while she comes over to join me. "It seems so much trouble for one life."

*

In the afternoon Maggie gets restless and her back hurts, so I massage it for her. There are tremendous knots at the base of her spine and on either side, over her pelvis.

She finds the massage relaxing, so I sit, crouched and cross legged behind her, so that she can be on her right side - her most comfortable position. I let my hand drift to her right seat bone where the cancer is a hard, hot lump, the size of half an orange. I cup it for a moment and stroke its dimensions. As I massage her lower back, in small circles, my hands and face get very hot, and the heat seems to transmit to Maggie, for when the matron comes in to take her temperature, it is high.

The matron says something to me and she sounds angry.

"You have to get off the bed," explains Maggie, "and sit on the chair. Visitors are not allowed on the bed."

The matron speaks again.

"She doesn't understand why people won't use the chairs. What is wrong with them?"

*

Maggie is restless and tearful all afternoon. Sometimes she dozes. She lies against the pillows with her eyes closed and licks her bottom lip with an odd grimace.

At about tea time she sits up. "I have to be sick. Get me a sheet."

I whip off the top sheet and hand it to her. She holds it under her chin and waits. Nothing happens.

"I want to be sick." She tries to retch, but nothing happens. She lies down again. More hours pass.

*

Maggie is much worse. She has more pain and it is more concentrated, in her lower back and left leg. There is a large swelling in her groin and she has lost more weight during the three weeks I have been in London.

Although she has injections of aspirin every six hours it doesn't help her much. I don't understand why they are not offering her anything stronger.

Evening comes. I decide to leave before nightfall as I anticipate trouble on the road back. As soon as Maggie had her evening medication and sleeping pill, I kiss her goodnight.

*

Sure enough, amid catcalls from the lorries thundering past, a man on a motorcycle stops just ahead of me. He takes his penis out and pulls it about - a sly smile on his face. In the dusk it gleams like a fat slug.

I sidle past him – and, averting my face, I trot up to the pensione, where a group of youths are gathered. They call out and jeer at me. I have to walk through them in dread that one of them might catch hold of me. Inside, the dining room is full of men playing cards.

I have no courage now - no spark of self-defense. The whole room pricks its ears at my approach and I have to walk through their stares.

I long for the return of Marco and Mateo. I lock the door and lie down with all my clothes on and fall asleep. When Marco wakes me, banging on the door, he seems surprised that the door is locked.

*

Maggie is up and about. As we step out of the lift we see her limp out of another patient's room.

"Caio."

I embrace her. Today is the first day of her new treatment.

We walk back towards the lift, where easy chairs delineate the waiting area. I sit cross-legged next to Maggie. She is indignant.

"Do you know, no fewer than three people thought you were my daughter!"

"Really? I can't imagine why."

"You jus' an ol' bag."

I study Maggie's face. It is true. Cancer has taken her age from her. Her face is smooth and yellow, the skin pulled taught over her cheek bones. Her eyes are brilliant, a clear blue-grey with fox-colored rings around the pupil. Hawk eyes.

"This cancer must have aged me thirty years."

"No, I don't think so, Maggie. People just don't understand why a friend would be with you, so they assume I am a close relation."

The matron comes by and shouts something over our heads.

"I am afraid you have to take your feet off the chair."

I put my feet down and glare at the matron, who says something else.

"She just doesn't understand what you have against chairs."

Maggie translates and assumes her mock innocent look.

"Fuck off."

Marco giggles.

*

It is time for her treatment and, ushered by the matron, we walk into a small room with a bed, dominated by a machine with six paws. These are heating filaments the size of soup plates, protected by plastic pads, filled with water. The matron helps Maggie onto the bed and places these pads around Maggie's behind, groin, and leg. Then she administers a Valium injection, covers Maggie with heavy blankets and leaves us to get on with it. The treatment is to take an hour and a half.

For the first half hour, Maggie remains cheerful. But the rest of the time is hell. She weeps and tosses her head from side to side. Marco fans her with the machine's operating manual, and I hold her hand and stroke her wrist and arm, wet with perspiration. Time crawls by. I try cold, wet compresses on her neck and forehead, but they don't help. She had been told to keep absolutely still, and except for her head and left arm she doesn't move a muscle. She takes off her head scarf to fan herself with, and I get my first view of her without hair.

Her forehead has no limit. Her naked pate gives her the air of a sick alien. Only her eyes, cheekbones, nose and lips give clues as to her identity.

The matron checks in and, seeing Maggie's distress, points to an air conditioner by my shoulder. Rough with eagerness, I turn the knob. The matron snaps at me.

"Don't break it," Marco translates.

Maggie asks me to recite her some more Monty Python.

"Do the Dead Parrot sketch."

"I can't Maggie, I just don't feel funny."

"Sing me Christmas carols then."

Bring me flesh and bring me wine, bring me pine logs hither.
Thou and I will see him dine, when we bear him thither.
Page and monarch forth they went, forth they went together,
Through the rude wind's wild lament, and the bitter weather.

*

At last it is over. When we pull off the heavy blankets she runs with sweat, her vest and nightgown drenched. We dab her off with handfuls of hospital tissue and then she gets very cold. We dress her in dry clothes and wrap her in a blanket.

Her wet pillow has a picture of Superman streaking across it, and swept with déjà vu I remember a dream I had, back in London:

I had found Maggie in the cellar of a hospital, buried in chalk, white and dying. Deeply distressed I had gone outside for a moment, just in time to see Superman zoom down from the sky and whisk a woman up into the clouds. I had woken up laughing.

*

Maggie wants to sleep so Marco takes me out for lunch at a local place, where workmen come for their mid-day meal.

Pordenone is an industrial zone. Men travel far from home to work here, staying at pensiones and eating out at places like this one. In a large dining room with tables set with white linen, a helpful waiter, discusses our choices with Marco, making suggestions. Unlike England, where lunch is a grudged affair, Italy takes two hours for a proper meal and treats the mid-day break seriously.

The food is delicious. We start with fried lambs' brains.

"Did you see that Indiana Jones film where they eat live monkey brains? It's a great delicacy in China. They trap it in a special table with a hole in the middle, pry off the top of its skull and scoop out its brains with silver spoons. Then they laugh at the faces it makes."

"To you this seems very cruel - but in China it is not cruel. They don' see animals the way you do."

"What about the monkey? Physical suffering is not a relative thing. Cruelty is cruelty."

"No it is not. The Chinese would think you very sentimental. You cannot be cruel to an animal, because it has to know you are being cruel to it. You can only be cruel to people."

"How can you say that? Suffering is as real to animals as it is to people."

"You are talking of values. What is cruel for you is not cruel for me. Cruelty depends on your awareness. The more aware you are, the more cruel you are."

*

Marco is tired after lunch, so we go back to the pensione. He lies down on his bed, and curls away from me on my bed, and falls asleep. I write this and wait for him to wake by himself. He needs rest.

Later, we go for a cappuccino in the old part of Town and find a small outdoor café. It is quiet here, away from the busy main street, and Marco talks of meditation.

"Meditation is very dangerous because it make you vulnerable to evil."

"Why?"

"Because when you meditate you take a journey inside and you get strong. Then you think you know everything, and that is when evil comes. It comes when you are open."

"Don't you believe that evil is relative - like cruelty?"

"No."

*

Hospital lunch today is risotto and steak with courgettes. Maggie hardly touches it and I sit down at her place at the table to eat what is left.

The woman from the next bed joins me. She spreads a napkin on her side of the table and lays out her own silver-ware, and water glass. Then she gets a bottle of wine from her bedside cupboard and pours it with gentle hands. There is no glug, blub, or air bubble, and the white cloth remains spotless. This is done with all the reverent ritual of a mass.

She tells us that this wine is produced by her son-in-law.

*

Maggie and I go down to the waiting area for a change of pace, where a woman discusses her own 'case' with Maggie. She taps her chest and her eyes are frightened and lost. Her husband gets out of the lift and, after a few words with Maggie, he escorts his wife back to her room.

"She thinks she has a virus on the lungs'. They tell her they can't diagnose exactly what it is. Everybody but her knows it's cancer."

"How terrible to put her on the cancer ward."

"Why?"

"Because she must know everyone is on this floor because they have cancer."

"Oh no, she is quite sure she is the only one who doesn't have it."

*

Maggie wants to sleep, so I go downstairs to a public bar for a cappuccino. Out of the blue, I feel an explosion in my chest. Startled, I look straight ahead and recognize it for what it is: love and warmth for Mateo.

I shut my book and go back upstairs.

*

Maggie is flushed and hot. I sit next to her on the bed and stroke her legs and back. She starts to cry, her head cradled on her right arm.

"I don't often think this, but I wonder sometimes, why me?"

She begins to sob and my tears start to fall too. They run down my face and a few drops fall onto her arm. Surprised, she looks up at me, her eyes streaming.

We both burst out laughing and put our arms around each other. I stroke her gently and hold her close to me as if she were my baby.

The woman in the next bed is astonished.

"Mangiare, mangiare," she urges us.

*

It's Maggie's birthday today. The eighteenth of June. She is thirty-seven.

We are all dreading her second treatment due this morning at eight o'clock. Marco found a magazine for her with full color pictures of Guernsey, advertising it as the ideal holiday island.

We arrive at the hospital at half past eight and Maggie has just begun to cook. Her face is bright when she sees us. Marco and the nurses sing "Happy Birthday" to her. But as she heats up, she begins to cry. She turns the pages of Marco's magazine roughly. It tears straight across a photo of St Peter Port Harbor, blue and cool. I take the magazine from her and fan her face. She weeps in Italian.

"What is it?" I ask.

"My mother didn't even kiss me when she was here for Easter."

Marco comes over "I know why."

"Why."

"Because she has very bad breath!"

Maggie pulls off her bandana. Her head is wet with perspiration.

"You know she love you. She jus' don' show her feelings, is all."

"I know. I know."

*

We drive into the old part of Pordenone to shop for Maggie's birthday. We stop outside a pastry shop and choose a cake, big enough for the nurses to share.

Across the street I see a flower shop selling pinks. They are in big bunches in buckets on the pavement. They used to grow in our garden and we used to call them Sweet William because of their scent.

*

Every afternoon before tea, before the kettle comes to a boil, Maggie and me go with Granny up the garden to give the hens corn. We run ahead, stopping only to sniff the clump of pinks that grow by the path. Feeding the hens is a treat for us, because we love to watch them rush out of their run on their Baba Yaga legs, scratch the earth and then back up to peck at the grass roots and grains of corn.

By the time we get back, after another ritual sniff of the Sweet William, the kettle will be boiling.

*

The old woman in the next bed left today so I lie in her place and fall into a deep sleep. I wake up standing on my feet in a state of shock. Someone is outside the door and I am sure it is the matron.

Maggie giggles at my bleary panic.

"You should see your face!"

"Fuck you, dear!"

*

Maggie gossips through the afternoon about Oriago: her neighbors, Catholic priests, schools, and Italians generally. She doesn't elaborate and assumes I know what she is talking about.

"I don't understand why, but Mateo is taking all this harder than Marco."

"'I suppose it is because he loves you, almost as if you were his own wife. Being a twin, and unmarried himself, you must seem closer than is usual for a sister-in-law."

"It's true. Sometimes I think I have two husbands. You don't know what it is like trying to go against the two of them."

"I can imagine."

*

In the evening, Marco returns, to take me for supper. We wait for Maggie's final injection, and then tuck her in. Marco puts his arms around her and she smiles into his face.

"Thank you for a lovely birthday."

He leans over her and kisses her on the lips, stroking her baldness under her scarf. She smiles and he giggles softly in Italian.

I watch them both. This is her last birthday. As I see them together, in rare harmony, I long for its continuance. I passionately want them both to be happy together for what is left. When Marco turns smiling, I hope my eyes are not catching the light.

"We go now, yes Anita."

"Yes." I kiss Maggie goodnight, and we leave.

*

Over supper as Marco and I talk again, over good wine, I feel another chord is being struck. I am not alarmed because I trust Marco and I know I can trust myself. But it upsets me. I don't know where I am anymore. None of my reactions are predictable. Either I feel nothing, or I fall in love with them all. When the barrier between life and death go down, all the other barriers go down too.

All the familiar landmarks are gone.

*

I wake up in tears to the sound of church bells. Mateo said he might come today, but he is so unpredictable in his comings and goings.

I ask Marco.

"He call before you 'wake. He come on Tuesday to take you back to Oriago."

Miserably disappointed, I have to acknowledge the well of loneliness, missing Mateo touches off in me. I don't know what the hell is going on. I just don't want to be in a world where I desire twin brothers. I never knew I was this immoral.

The church bells ring on.

*

Time is flying by.

Mateo is coming tomorrow to take me back to Oriago. Even though my flight is booked for Thursday, he can only get the day off to drive me on Tuesday. So I'll have to kick my heels with Maria and the girls on Wednesday.

Today Maggie had another treatment, and another is due tomorrow. I can't bear the thought of leaving her at the hospital's mercy.

In my mind's eye I watch Maggie toss and turn in her bright yellow bandana, either complaining or crying. The hollows of her cheekbones have stretched back into pools of shadow in front of her ears. Her skull is beginning to show. I see her curled on her bed and hear her little 'ah's' as I rub her back. Her bottom is an emaciated bag of marbles. The pain is spreading.

It feels as if there is no flesh on my heart - no rib cage between us, as its strange, improper yearnings try to touch and unite with hers. I love her.

*

"I do love you Maggie, " as we walk together towards the treatment room.

She smiles and leans her head on my shoulder and I put my arm around her shoulder to give her a hug. She is so weak I overbalance us both, and we fall, laughing together, against the wall.

*

She lies, calm and dozy, and speaks the odd word or sentence. Sometimes she forgets I don't speak Italian, or speaks so low, I can't hear her.

*

An old woman with Hodgkin's' comes down to Maggie's room for a visit. As I lie on the forbidden bed, I take hold of her hand, which she accepts as quite natural. For a while, I let myself sink into her greater age as she stands next to Maggie. She talks and smiles and nods her trembling head, occasionally squeezing my hand.

Her eyes are holy – gold and luminous – like eagle eyes.

*

Marco suffers. He keeps busy. He runs lots of errands and makes lots of phone calls.

Tonight, I tackle him about Maggie.

"Marco, I think we must think of Maggie dying, rather than treating her as if she is going to live. We must prepare for her death, so that she can die as comfortably as possible and keep her dignity."

"Do you think so Anita?"

Both he and Mateo have pale, almost invisible blond eyebrows under their red curly hair. Combined with their blue eyes it gives them a naked look that can be either hostile or intensely vulnerable.

I feel I have gone too far and stop.

"The doctor tell me today, that the cancer has spread to her brain."

"Oh."

"Her other leg begin to hurt her now."

"Yes I know."

What is to be done? What can we do?

*

I know Mateo has arrived, when, during Maggie's treatment, my heart begins to gallop. Sure enough, a few minutes later, he walks in and greets us all.

"Ciao, Anita." He smiles at me and I am overwhelmed by shyness.

When it is time to go, Marco goes out onto the balcony, and stares out over the fields. They are lovely in the evening light, almost ready for harvest, under the skimming swallows, and a rising full moon. I put my arms about him and he hugs me back.

"I must go now."

"Si Anita."

Inside, Maggie plays indifferent to our parting. She waves from the bed.

"Bye, Anita."

"Goodbye, Maggie."

Marco sees me to the door and kisses me goodbye.

*

Mateo jokes in the lift on the way down.

"In America, most rapes take place in the lifts, between the floors."

The lift descends at a snail's pace.

*

On the road back it is dark. The full moon floats alongside our car - serene and unbearable. I thought my tears were hidden by the night and engine noise, but I was wrong.

Mateo pulls up to a gas station and holds my hand. I start to weep in earnest, and he pulls me to him. I sob into his neck. He rubs the back of my head, and then, firmly pushing my hair out of the way, he holds my face and kisses me.

"Eh, Anita," he says as I slow down, "you English."

"You Italians," I reply.

His eyes are soft. "So, you are human."

"But you know that," I reply, angry again.

*

Mateo takes me and the little girls to the beach again. It is hot, with thunder in the air. I dive down and stalk Daisy and Chloe in the underwater gloom. They shriek as I tickle their feet.

Back on the beach, we all sunbathe, and Mateo notices that I am reading a book on American feminists.

"They don' understand what it is like for a man. We work like pigs. They only talk about it because is fashionable. They understand nothing. They don' know wha' it is like when you have to work. Women do not have to work. They can choose. Men work like pigs their whole life."

"A lot of women have to work like pigs their whole life too."

"Not women like you. You can choose no?"

"Well, yes, now I can, but..."

"If you had to work like a man, you wouldn't wan' to be a liberated woman."

"Just a minute…" I'm not about to be called shallow.

"You think you can find life in a book, but it is not like that. When you work every day of your life, you find out what life is like."

He is infuriated too.

I gape at him - his stupidity — his pompous self-centered rhetoric.

He drives us home and leaves immediately to see his girlfriend. I didn't know he had a girlfriend. No one told me. Now I am jealous as well as insulted.

I want him to kiss me again.

*

The phone rings. It is Marco. Maria and Viola talk over my head, faces grave and anxious.

"What has happened?"

Viola gives me the phone. Marco is in a panic.

"Anita, she cannot walk any more. Her legs don' hold her. She nearly in a coma. She much worse. We bring her home tomorrow. They say no more treatments."

"I'll wait for you here. I won't go back yet."

"What about Andy?"

"He'll have to cope. This is an emergency."

"Yes, I think it is."

*

"Tell Daddy to give me ten pence a day."

"I love you mummy. I want you back, but I don't know how to dial your number."

Andy's voice is cold. "We are all disappointed. The kids will be very disappointed."

My voice is cold too. "I love you, and I miss you." I say - and hope it is still true.

*

Maggie is dressed and curled up on the bed, impatient as ever, to be gone before her energy flags.

"Did Andy go mad?"

"Sort of."

When Marco brings a wheel chair to the side of her bed, Maggie heaves herself upright. She refuses his help and claws into the seat by herself.

"Can I push you?"

"Yes. You push me."

But the wheel chair has a life of its own. It won't go into a straight line, and weaves us along the corridor to the lift, and Maggie weeps.

Outside the lift, the old woman with the golden, eagle eyes. Her face is all love.

"Va bene," she says. "Go well."

Downstairs the wheel chair takes unto pillars and dusty rubber plants. Maggie is very patient, but when we go outside, and there is a steep ramp down, to where the ambulance is waiting, she stiffens, gripping the arm rests with her thin hands.

"You do realize it could all end - right here."

"Yes I do."

The ambulance men lift her onto a sliding stretcher, push her in. Marco, who must stay behind to wind up affairs, wishes us goodbye.

*

We drive round corners. Maggie winces in pain but once we are on the open road, she goes into a doze. She holds onto my leg.

My mind, with nowhere else to go, swims us back to Guernsey. Like the wheelchair I can't seem to feel or think in a straight line.

Maggie's gate creaks as she comes come out of her house. I am waiting for her in the lane. Together we walk, as we have so many times, all during our childhood and adolescence, down towards Saints Bay.

See, Maggie, see the green hedges thick with ragged robin. See here, the crossroads where the bus can take us right into town, or left, where we used to walk to school together - you in tears if I had made us late. Feel how the hill turns down to the sea as we come abreast of the Saints Bay Tea Garden.

Let us go in to look at the orange fish in their fountain, and the big wheel of stone that crushed the grain before we were born. The millstone is our secret that only we know and we never pass by without paying homage in the gloom of its outhouse.

And see the cattle trough where our dogs drink and you eat the nasturtiums gone wild, and we can hear the stream as it picks up momentum with the hill, and let us step over the cobbled groove, where it crosses the road, shallow and clear. Here we enter the cool tree-corridor, where eucalyptus grows, littering the road with its seeds, giving off its childhood, cold-curing smell.

Now we pass the narrow place with room for only a few cars to park, shivering in the heat and smelling of petrol, opposite the turning to Fisherman's Harbor, where once we saw them bring in a drowned man, wrapped in canvas with one arm dangling.

This is the last bit where the hill is very steep. The stream is big now, gurgling deep in the undergrowth, and we arrive by the tiny shack that serves tea in tomato baskets. Let us pass onto the slip-way built for fishermen's boats, and past the bright floats, piled up for visitors. We step out onto the pebbles - but now, since we have no weight, there is no sound of shingle - only the sigh of the sea and the call of gulls. There is no-one on the beach but us, because we are ghosts. We walk onto the wet sand at the water's edge and watch the seaweed heave in the shallows, loosened by deep sea storms and fishermen's work.

Here is a white quartz pebble lying in its own sandy hollow and you pick it up, wet and white, while the next wave soothes out its resting place. Gently you stroke it with your thumb that bends back at the knuckle, and you put it in your pocket, glad you found it first.

As ghosts, we are free to walk on and submerge ourselves, alive, onto the seabed. Dark weed climbs over our heads and, in the clear water, we can see the knees of the cliffs, shifting with the waves and fishermen's ropes. Fishes tremble like the first touch of lips, curious, not sure of what they are seeing, best friends, on the sea floor, seeking comfort.

*

Daisy is eleven years old today.

Everyone is here: Daisy and Chloe. Maria, Marco, and Viola, with Mateo due soon. Many more people are invited. I dread this birthday party which is planned for the afternoon. Maggie lies on the couch in the living room, so she can be part of the preparations. Marco and I prepare sandwiches at the dining room table. As usual, she criticizes everything we do.

"There is too much butter. You mustn't do it that way. Go and get a proper knife from the kitchen."

'Shut up, you old bag, and let us get on with it'.

Maggie's face registers neither humor nor anger. But she seems to relax.

When we are done, I sit next to her and gently knead her back and stroke her bottom.

Tears seep through her closed eyes. "Everything is so black."

"You know, don't you, that you are more than the blackness."

"Yes." She nods, but keeps her eyes closed.

"What are you thinking about?"

"Oh," she opens her eyes, "so many things bother me – little things - stupid things."

"Is it because you don't want to think of the big thing?"

"Yes." She nods again and closes her eyes once more.

*

Daisy's party is held in the garden, so that Maggie can be alone on the couch if she wants. Although she is in a lot of pain today, she rises to the occasion. People come in at intervals all through the afternoon to gossip. Maggie laughs and smiles and I sit by her feet with her little mongrel dog, Georgia. At one point she even manages to hobble into the garden with a blanket draped about her shoulders. I support her to a table, laden with half eaten food, half-filled wine bottles, and the rubble of a birthday cake.

I watch everyone's smiles of welcome become fixed, as, in the sunlight, Maggie's terminal condition becomes clear. She looks like Nosferatu in a bandana.

*

"Maggie, I would like to sleep with you tonight, if it's okay with you. I'd really like to, and Marco needs rest."

"Yes," she agrees, almost offhand.

Except when she was in hospital, all through these months, Maggie and Marco have stuck together at night. Maggie is most afraid of being alone at night, and Marco is at his most defensive about leaving her to others.

Maggie is in the spare room, and it has two single beds. Marco has found a portable toilet for her. It is night. The light is warm and golden, and our shadows on the wall, orange.

"We've decided to sleep together," I say to Marco. Maggie smiles with her eyes. We have become conspirators again.

"You sleep downstairs and get a good night's rest."

"Okay," he smiles too. He is much too tired to argue or worry about me, or Maggie.

*

Maggie wakes up in pain at two o'clock I make up a powder for her, prescribed by the hospital. The moon is so bright that I don't need to turn on the light. As I sit next to her on her bed we are splashed with pale blue moonbeams. When she has finished her potion I put her empty glass onto the floor and it disappears into a pool of ink.   She asks me to sing to her.

Black girl, Black girl, don't you lie to me,
Where did you sleep last night?

In the pines, in the pines, where the sun never shines,
I shivered the whole night through.

*

Marco takes me to the bar up the road for a cappuccino.

It is a short walk with the usual lunatic drivers swooping past. Marco shows me a safe way and we climb down the embankment into a field of American corn. Already it is taller than we are, and it clicks in the breeze, over our heads. Maggie will be dead before it is reaped, and this knowledge turns it into brass. My mind insists that it must be made of a permanent material.

*

Today is voting day as well as Sunday. Outside, there is a loud stream of bonnet-to-boot traffic on its way to the voting booth, church, or beach. By the afternoon, for one reason or another, the whole family is away, and I am alone with Maggie.

There is a knock on the front door.

"You'd better see who it is."

A little nervous, I go downstairs. There are so many people on the road, and I am afraid of an intruder whose language I don't speak.

I open the door onto an old man, crippled by a hunched back. His face, down at the level of my waist, is brown as a nut and deeply lined.

"Buon giorno, Seignor," I say, hoping I'll understand his reply.

But of course, I don't. He looks at me out of almost black eyes and says something.

"Non parlo italiano," I counter.

He stays put and repeats what he just said. He seems to be quite sure that he belongs just where he stands.

"Un momento, per favore." Leaving the door open, I rush upstairs.

"Maggie, there's a man downstairs, with a hunched back, and I don't know what he is saying."

"Oh Lord. It's Aurelio! He's Marco's uncle. He comes every Sunday for a meal. They've all forgotten. Tell him to come up."

I go back out of the room, but Aurelio is already at the bottom of the stairs taking his shoes off. He has come in and shut the door behind him. I beckon to him and he climbs slowly up. In Maggie's room, I find him a chair, and he sits down on the edge, his feet in brown socks, his toes just touching the floor.

"Can I get him something Maggie? Some coffee, perhaps?"

"No. He'll want Grappa."

When I return he is deep in conversation with Maggie. I hand him the Grappa and climb on the bed with Maggie to rub her back. I can tell when she is hurting. I watch Aurelio as he talks to her. He nods his head for emphasis and moves his hands in slow, curling waves.

Maggie nods back with an occasional "ah," or "oh." They are mirrors to one another in some way I can't reach, but only sense.

*

After supper, Marco goes up to be with Maggie. I take a break and go for a cappuccino walking the safe way, past the brass corn.

To be with Maggie in her dying time is essentially impossible. My mind reels away from the reality. I am too alive to be with Maggie as she dies, the way Aurelio can.

*

It was my turn to be with Maggie last night. Marco and I are taking alternate nights now. She hardly sleeps at all. She dozes for about two hours and then awakes in pain. I turn on the light and prepare her another powder. When she takes it, I turn out the light again and sit next to her on the bed.

"Do you remember Gunner, next door's dog?"

I can feel her smile in the dark.

"Do you remember his trick, when we wanted to leave him behind and he wanted to follow us? We'd say *Stay!* and he'd fall on the ground as if all his legs broke at once, his tail between his legs and tears in his eyes. The old hypocrite! The moment we were round the corner out of sight, he'd thunder after us, and if we told him to *Go home Gunner!* he'd try to commit suicide under the next passing car until we had to rescue him. Then he'd wag his tail and grin because he'd be officially with us."

"Tell me more."

"Remember when we took him on the cliffs, and he'd chase the rabbits under the gorse. All you'd see were the bushes waving as he tore after them. We'd be clanking with bottles of water for him because there was none down on the beach. His water weighed more than our lunches."

When the powder takes effect, she begins to wander.

"What a funny time to have a Flebo."

She thinks she is getting a glucose drip.

*

"I hate waking up. It's always the same."

I stroke her arm. The pain killers are inadequate. Marco has been to three doctors to try and find one that is effective. I want her to have morphine, but she resists the idea.

"I will need it later, if the pain gets worse."

Marco and I feel she is losing ground fast. She eats nothing at all now, and complains of weakness, and always, more pain.

*

The last few days have all run together. I don't know how Marco did it for so long, alone. It is impossible to get any sleep. She is in great pain now, cannot get off the bed at all, except to go to the portable toilet. Her pain has spread to her gut, and we are all afraid. What is going to happen?

Marco is out every day. He visits traditional doctors as well as homeopathic healers in an attempt to find an effective pain killer. No one will come to the house.

They all insist Maggie must go back into hospital. The
skin on Marco's face is stretched and white.

Today he is out again, trying again to get a doctor to
come to the house so that morphine can be prescribed.

The drugs he has managed to get so far are useless.
They knock her out for about three hours, and then the
pain slowly begins to build. Then she has an aspirin
injection to hold her until her next knock out dose,
three hours after that.

I have learned to prepare the aspirin injections, and
Maria, who learnt to inject her husband when he was ill,
administers them. Maria runs the house, and I keep the
clock for Maggie's medication. When it is time, and I
have filled the syringe, I go downstairs to the kitchen, to
call her.

"Maria, viene."

She nods with a smile and wipes her hands on a towel.

"Si, Anita, andiamo."

Maria's smile lights up her eyes with a kind of fierce
recognition of you as someone who needs her
attention. She smiles with all her teeth and usually has a
humorous remark to go with it. She once said of me:

The great thing about Anita is that you can put her in a hole and leave her there.

Once upstairs, Maria asks for the alcohol, and carefully pours it over her hands. Then I hand her the syringe, and, with her fore and middle fingers, she finds the spot on the fleshy part of Maggie's hip, separates her fingers, and slips the needle in. Then, very carefully, with both hands, she pushes in the plunger. Maggie lies on one side or the other and licks her top teeth with her tongue. Bedsores have appeared on her hips.

Maggie's English friends come by every day and she rallies a little for them, but she is in too much pain. She either moans or dozes and it is difficult for them to remain cheerful.

Once, three of them came at once. "Put on the parrot sketch, Anita," Maggie asks me.

"They must listen to Monty Python."

I put on the cassette for them.

Look, matey, I know a dead parrot when I see one, and I'm looking at one right now.

No, no, he's not dead, he's restin'! Remarkable bird, the Norwegian Blue, idn'it, ay? Beautiful plumage!

The plumage don't enter into it. It's stone dead.

Maggie hisses quietly with her eyes closed. I watch three appalled women sitting tidily on the other bed. I don't know whether to laugh with Maggie, or to look shocked with them - as if Maggie's gone off her rocker.

*

Maggie with Marco, in post-shot relief. Rye Cooder is on the cassette machine.

Every woman I know, is crazy 'bout an automobile,
And here I am standing
With nothing but rubber heels...

"I want to dance."

Marco helps her to her feet and supports her as he gently sways from side to side. Her bald head is nestled into his neck as they smooch, her hands limp on his shoulders. Suddenly she bursts into tears.

"You know I have always been a bad dancer," says Marco, "bu' there is no need to cry."

Maggie smiles up at him, through her tears, as he puts her back to bed, and covers her with a sheet.

*

Marco washes Maggie with soap and a face cloth. She winces and frowns.

"It's cold Marco. I'm cold."

A frown between his eyes, with great care, he rubs the washcloth over her belly and breasts, under-arms, and shoulders. Water falls from the wrung-out cloth, into the basin, like bursts of rain against a window.

When he leaves with the soapy, tepid water, Maggie says:

"Grazie, Marco."

From the door, basin under his arm, he smiles into her eyes.

"Prego," he replies.

*

Mildred, Maggie's mother, telephones from Guernsey. I speak to her in Marco and Maggie's old bedroom. Maria sleeps here now with Viola.

"Maggie can't get to the phone."

"Is she very bad?"

"Yes, I'm afraid she is."

Mildred begins to cry. "I'm glad you're there."

*

This morning Maggie asks Marco, "Help me to die."

He goes still with shock. It is impossible for him to give up.

*

I massage Maggie's back. She's better today - reminiscing about the past.

At nineteen and eighteen, we visited my new hippie boyfriend in North Wales.

"My God," remembers Maggie, "they gave us this terrible stew, full of potatoes and beans. It was supposed to be healthy. The next day I had to take this huge shit, and they had this ghastly outside toilet, in the middle of a bog, and I was in there for hours, in a howling gale."

We begin to laugh and laugh. Helpless, with tears streaming down our faces, we weave from side to side, and Maggie bangs the covers with her hand.

"... and your face, when you had to wash in that stream."

"Jesus Christ! I'd forgotten. They had no plumbing at all, and we all had to wash in the stream outside. The water was so cold that, as soon as I put my hands in, pain shot up my arms into my armpits like lightning bolts. It was agony."

Marco and Mateo come in to see what all the noise is about. We are speechless – whimpering with mirth. Pleased, but baffled, they leave us to our gaiety.

*

Maggie cries. "Chloe, Daisy," she whispers into her pillow.

I put my arms around her and kiss her. "I know, I know."

"Chloe came in with a book this morning, but I couldn't stay with her to the end of it. She was so enthusiastic, but I was so tired."

I wish this dying could get into the open, so that I can speak directly to her, so that I can try and share the separation and loss she is going through – the terrible grief of her burden.

I am ashamed of myself - at my stupid passions and childish cowardice. For being alive, in fact.

*

A doctor finally comes and prescribes morphine, but it doesn't work any better than the other drugs. He told Marco that Maggie is one of the worst cases he has ever seen.

Before him, another doctor came to the house, but he sat outside in his car for a moment before he drove away. Even the professionals are afraid of Maggie's pain, because there is no end to it, only more.

*

Daisy is frightened to go upstairs alone.

Marco has decided Maggie must go back into hospital.

*

Today, as Marco washes Maggie, she starts to weep.

"I have got nothing."

"What do you mean - nothing?"

But Maggie cannot answer - continues to cry.

"Is it because you are afraid to lose Marco?"

"Yes." She nods. Tears stream down her face.

"I feel as if I am going to die soon."

Marco holds her close and strokes and kisses her wet face.

"I don't want to be buried; I want to be cremated."

"Why?"

"More hygienic."

"But when you go to the earth, you go to your mother."

"I want my ashes scattered on the sea."

"What's wrong with the earth?"

But she smiles now, and looks into Marco's eyes, and strokes his hair.

"The sea is a different kind of mother. Maggie's thinking about the sea around Guernsey."

"Si." Maggie nods.

A vivid flash of Fisherman's harbor where we saw the poor drowned boy bought in. I have an urn of her ashes in my hands.

I begin to cry too and stroke her leg. Maggie holds my hand.

"Daisy," she whispers, "Chloe." She cries again.

Separation is the worst pain, I want to say, but Marco says:

"Anyway, we going to cure you."

Maggie nods up at him, smiling, her arm around his neck.

*

Marco calls Alitalia, to find out when the next flight back to London will be.

"You must go back to Andy and the kids. They need you."

But there is no seat free for another week. Mateo, next to me, bursts out laughing, and throws his arms around me.

"You won' be home 'til Christmas!"

*

Marco has found a place in the local hospital at Treviso. She is to go in tomorrow.

"She cannot die here, with the children."

I disagree. I think that the children should go somewhere else, until it is all over. But I say nothing. Marco is exhausted. He has to orchestrate everything himself in a tightening circle of calamity. He asks me to break the news to her.

"No!" Then she whispers: "I knew they were up to something."

"Maggie, we can't look after you properly here. Your pain still isn't under control, and you need a Flebo to bring you up. You aren't eating anything."

"It's true I need a Flebo."

*

Mateo takes me to the local bar, and buys me a glass of sparkling, white wine. Close to him – feeling his body heat - I yearn to lose myself in his sex. I long to blot all this out in orgasm after orgasm.

*

I oversleep and awake to find that the children have gone. Marco found a seaside flat for them, and they have left for a summer "holiday" with Viola. Marco's arrangements are like this. You often find out after the fact what he has organized.

Today we will take Maggie back to hospital. Maggie is up and dressed, impatient to be off.

"Why are they taking so long? They were supposed to be here half an hour ago."

She is on the bed, curled on her left side in trousers and blouse that hang away from her frame. Her baldness is covered, as usual, by a yellow head scarf. She frowns and licks her bottom lip. She hasn't had her morphine yet, because we know how painful the move is going to be for her.

"We give it to her just before she leave," says Marco.

Finally, we hear the wheels crunch on the gravel outside. Maria and I have been poised to give her the injection as soon as we hear the ambulance. I hand Maria a cotton swab and the alcohol for her hands, and she slips the needle into Maggie's rump.

Two ambulance men come upstairs into the room with a kind of rubber sheet with handles which they put onto the floor. Maria leaves, as they gently ease Maggie down onto it. Maggie winces and gasps. Her teeth bite down on her bottom lip.

"Pian, pian," I say, getting in their way.

With infinite care, and soft smiles to me and Maggie, they ease her round the door. Maggie's face is filled with anxiety, and she clutches at the banisters grimacing at the pain.

"No, signora," they tell her softly. "Let us do the work."

Standing next to Maria, at the bottom of the stairs, I see how small Maggie has become. By the front door they put her onto a hard stretcher and start to angle her out of the house. Maria bursts into tears and runs into the back of the house, followed by Marco. For her, this is goodbye.

Outside, neighbors from across the road, and next door, wait in the garden.

"Brava Maggie, brava."

"Please go with her, Anita," says Marco.

I get in the ambulance and sit down next to a young nurse, opposite Maggie, and we drive off. Maggie falls into a doze, and, as we turn corners, the nurse leans forward to hold Maggie against any unnecessary jolts.

I stare out of the back window, and soon Marco and Mateo follow us, in separate cars, one behind the other, unsmiling, anxious mirrors of each other.

The ambulance men wheel out the stretcher and push her into Emergency Outpatients. Marco has had to wangle her into hospital this way. They won't accept her as a cancer patient, so she must come in on an emergency basis, as if all this has just happened. As if we have just noticed.

We are left together in the middle of a large room, with people on chairs arranged around the wall. They look at us in silence. Maggie is the only one there who is not ambulatory.

"I have peed myself." She struggles not to cry.

"Don't worry Maggie. We'll soon get you comfortable. As soon as Marco and Mateo get here. Hold on just a little longer."

I lean over to kiss her - stroke her head. Everyone looks away, except for three nuns, who look on, amazed.

By the time the brothers arrive, she is desperate, and Marco rushes over to a passing doctor.

"Not in here," wails Maggie, "not in the waiting room."

"Of course not. They'll take you somewhere. Try not to worry."

The doctor comes over, unsmiling, and starts to wheel Maggie away.

"Stay with her, Anita," says Marco.

I walk beside Maggie, my hand on her arm, through corridors and swing doors, until we arrive in an anteroom. The doctor is joined by a nurse, and they prepare to push Maggie through a door. I follow, but the doctor glares at me and puts up his hand, in front of my chest.

His air is one of outrage. I fume outside, listening for the smallest groan, the merest whimper, and fantasize rushing in and punching him on the nose, smacking his self-righteous face. But, when Maggie comes out, she is smiling and relieved.

"They were really kind. They cleaned me up and everything."

We roll back to the main waiting room, and I realize that the doctor was just as anxious as we are. It is so hard to accept that doctors are as afraid of death as anyone else.

Marco and Mateo are nowhere to be seen. Obviously, they are somewhere filling out forms. Maggie is comfortable now as I lean against her stretcher and stroke her leg.

"I think those nuns think we are a little more than just friends."

Maggie chuckles. "They've just got dirty minds."

Marco walks in with another doctor, and they wheel Maggie away. I sit down next to Mateo who is completely silent. He sits with his hands dangled between his knees; his head bowed.

I stroke the springy ginger hair on his forearm. The nun's eyes are popping. They are quite right. My amorality is bottomless.

*

Upstairs, we are ushered into another waiting room, and Maggie is wheeled away, to be put to bed. Marco comes in with an English woman.

"Hello, my name is Harriet. My mother is here, and it looks as if they are going to put Maggie next to her. They can keep one another company since they are both English."

Harriet is pretty, bright and blond.

"What's wrong with your mother?"

"She was taken ill while she was visiting me.

She felt ill before she left, actually, but she wouldn't go to the doctor in England. They've diagnosed cancer of the spleen. She came over here even though she felt very ill."

"How dreadful for you."

"Yes. But it is all Karma, you understand."

I am silent, but see Marco, who has his own ideas, curl his lip.

"She teach yoga over here," he explains to me.

"Oh."

"Yes. And I've learned a lot about fate. If you do Yoga regularly you can't help but know about Karma, you understand."

"Yes, I suppose that's true. Are they going to operate on your mother?"

"Yes they are. But you understand she's got jaundice. They'll operate as soon as that's cleared up. She's on a Flebo, to detoxify her. That's a drip, you understand."

I nod. "I know all about Flebos"

"Her spleen doesn't work, so she's got to be detoxified, you understand. I can't leave her for a minute because she keeps pulling out the Flebo. She's a naughty old girl. I've had to be here all night. I can't leave her."

A nurse comes in and says something to Marco.

"Maggie is ready now." he tells us.

We all troop down the corridor, onto a small ward, the farthest away, again, from the nurse's station. Inside, Maggie is with three other women. She is settled and seems comfortable. She turns her head towards a woman in the next bed.

"This is Harriet. Harriet, this is Anita, my friend from England."

I move over to the old lady's side who is, indeed - bright yellow. As I stand next to her, I can feel her fever. She has an intravenous bottle attached to her arm. Her hands pluck at the bedclothes.

"Hello Harriet, how are you feeling?"

"I couldn't half go a nice eggs and bacon with sausage. I haven't eaten in five days."

Harriet junior leans against the window with her arms folded.

"You stick to your Flebo, like a good girl."

"Humph."

"You're both called Harriet."

"Yes. But I call her Hattie."

We stay there the rest of the afternoon. Marco talks with Hattie and I sit with Maggie and Harriet. Harriet dozes off, and I can see that in her sleep she indeed picks at the Flebo. As she tosses and turns, she is always in danger of pulling it out.

*

We take turns with Maggie and Harriet - resting in shifts. Hattie stays with them at night, and Marco and I stay with them in the daytime.

It is absolutely necessary that someone be with them all the time, as the nurses completely ignore us. Any time I go down to the nurse" station to call one for help, they tut or look blank. We are known as the Ingleses, and they joke about us behind our backs.

I become efficient with padellas (bedpans) as well as untangling and changing Harriet's Flebo. She, in particular, needs a lot of attention. She has to pee often because the drip is flooding her system with liquid.

She wakes up suddenly and says: "I've got to go," and I dive around her bed with a padella, and lifting her, sling it under her bottom.

She is very grateful. "You're a proper duck you are."

Maggie uses the padella as well, but her pee is an orange, oily smear.

*

There are four beds. Harriet is nearest the wall, then Maggie, and next to her an old woman who broke her back. She is incarcerated in plaster, with a Chinese kimono on top that gives her a circus air. Next to her is a woman with lank, dark hair. She is suffering from paralysis of the legs that has no apparent cause. She says nothing, but looks ahead of her, unsmiling and sad.

The woman with the broken back has taken it upon herself to keep the ward in order. She gives out advice and orders. Harriet can't abide her.

"She don't share nothing."

It is true. All the patients have a locker against the wall near the window. The woman with the broken back has a treasure trove in hers: boxes of chocolates and bottles of wine. This is more than Harriet can bear, in her starved condition, watching her dig into her hoard - offering none to anyone else.

We watch her toddle painfully over to her locker and pour herself a glass of wine. With her back to us, she quaffs it with great difficulty, due to the cast, tottering on her heels.

"You do realize," I tell Harriet, "that she is a secret drinker. That must be how she broke her back. She tipped her head too far back and fell over backwards."

Harriet chuckles.

"Shut up, Anita'" hisses Maggie. "She speaks English."

"We don't care," snaps Harriet in a loud voice. She glares at the woman with the broken back, who sticks her nose in the air.

*

They have put Maggie on an oral medication which is at last doing the trick. Although it still hurts her to move, she is generally more comfortable, and less depressed. It is a great relief for her to have no more injections.

Her face is thinner. The shadows on her temples and behind her cheekbones are deeper than before. They seem to grow a little every day.

In the heat, she has abandoned her headscarf for once and for all and her lips don't quite meet, so that her front teeth are always visible. Her belly is dreadfully swollen. Apparently, cancer makes a liquid around itself. On her first day in, they give her an enema, which reduces the size a little. But they don't offer to do it again, even though her belly is now, just as swollen as before.

I tell her she is on morphine, and she begins to cry. For her, morphine, like wheelchairs and incontinence, is one more obvious step towards her inevitable end. Marco is angry with me.

"You should not have done that, Anita."

"It is better that she hear it from me, than from one of those stupid nurses."

Anyway Maggie denies it. "You won't get morphine out of them. Not here."

*

One evening, when our patients are more comfy than usual, Hattie and her husband invite Marco and I out for a pizza. We jump at the chance, and we all go to a nearby café. Marco's face is bleached and thin, and he always wears dark glasses now. Behind them, his eyes are blank and full of pain.

Harriet launches into a long dissertation about her yoga classes and other esoterica. I am too tired to join in and just listen — but find myself watching Marco.

To begin with, he just looks at her and acts as if he doesn't understand anything she is saying. And then, to my surprise, he asks her questions that he perfectly well knows the answers to.

"Excuse me, please, but what is Karma?" "I do not understand. What is yoga for?"

This gets Hattie more and more wound up. Then his questions became more and more searching until, with all the rope he gives her, she hangs herself on her ignorance. Then, he let it be known in a vague sort of way, that he's read a few books. He then disappears into a mysterious silence and refuses to be drawn further.

Later, back at the hospital, Hattie tells me: "That's a smart boy, believe me. Those still waters run deep."

This is precisely the impression he wants to convey, and it just makes me want to kick him.

*

Marco and I go out together every evening after Maggie is settled for the night. We relax over wine and good food, talk and laugh together with a kind of gallows humor.

He talks constantly about Maggie and their life together. She is a big enigma to him. I find this surprising because, to me, Maggie has always been an open book.

"She never say what she is feeling," is his constant puzzle.

I relish these times with Marco. If it wasn't for the fact that he is Maggie's husband, I'd be in far deeper water than I already am.

Instead, I enjoy infuriating him, and undercutting his game of Socratic ignorance. On a late-night drive home, I decide to teach him a lesson for his hypocritical performance with Hattie.

"The really great gift I have," I say - solemn enough, "the truly greatest gift, is that I am really humble."

This renders him nearly speechless. Humility, wisdom, grace are all virtues that, to Marco, by their nature, are unattainable ideals. He nearly drives into a hedge.

"You canno' be serious!"

"Oh yes I am. Only a fool doesn't acknowledge their true gifts."

"'Jesus Christ! You really are arrogant."

I smile into the darkness.

*

Marco and Mateo carve up life between them.

Mafia like, they divide it out into sections, and each one owns and relishes a particular aspect. Mateo is the bachelor: outgoing, openly sexual, and flamboyant - the doer and seducer of women. Marco is the thinker, the philosopher and poet who reflects and measures outcome and value - the one who suffers. Yet, each can vicariously enjoy the other's experience, and obtain it, psychically, second hand.

The trouble with this though, is that each shuts out a part of his own life for the other. Mateo behaves as if he is stupider than he is, and Marco as if he is less passionate.

Maggie has said: "It's like having two husbands, Anita. You don't know what it's like to have to go against them both."

And Mateo has said, more than once: "Maggie is more than a wife to me."

They are both losing the woman they love, severally and together. And neither of them can get close to her because each has shut down a part of himself, for the other.

*

One day Maggie wets herself while the doctors are examining her. We are out of the room, because they won't let us in when they are with their patients. The matron is there also, a forbidding lay nun, and she tells Maggie not to be a baby.

When we are allowed to go in, Maggie is crying uncontrollably. When Marco hears what has happened, he turns white with fury, and goes to follow the nun, to give her a piece of his mind.

"No, no. I have to live with her when you are not here, no?"

Marco turns back, and together we lean over her, to soothe and comfort her humiliation.

"They are not going to do a cure here. I know they're not."

"Are you afraid this is the end?" I ask her.

"Yes." Her voice wails in fear.

"Well," I whisper, "I'm afraid it might be."

Marco turns away but I pull him back by his sleeve. We sit on either side and hold her in our arms. She cries some more, and I cry as well. The truth is too much.

Then she reaches up and strokes our hair. She smiles at us, affection and sadness shine out of her wet eyes.

"Does my mother know? Is she coming?"

"I'll call her," says Marco.

We both know already that Mildred will not come. It is too much for her to bear. *I want to remember her how she was,* she has told Marco over the phone.

*

Later, Hattie asks me outside to speak with an English-speaking doctor who takes her yoga classes.

He tells me, "That was very cruel of you - to tell her she is dying."

"Do you really think, Maggie doesn't know she is dying?"

"Even so…" begins Hattie, but my face forbids her to continue.

The doctor looks uncomfortable, and they talk about Harriet and her operation, due soon.

I light a cigarette and look out of the window feeling like Maggie's executioner.

*

On my last day, Maggie insists that I come in early to wash her. She likes me to do this for her every morning, even though Marco is much better at it. I always manage to bump into her bad leg and cause her pain. Clumsy as usual, I cannon into the side of the bed.

"What you see is what you get, "I laugh.

Marco laughs too. "Christ, you clumsy."

But Maggie is grumpy and bad-tempered.

"I don't want that vest. That's the wrong soap. The water's cold."

"Maggie, you mustn't feel abandoned," I say, and she bursts into tears.

The doctors come in with the nun-matron and insist we leave. They are a long time, and it is soon time for me to catch my plane. Marco goes in to ask them if I can say goodbye.

In front of three embarrassed doctors and the matron, who looks on with a kind of sardonic enjoyment, as if the carryings on of us mere mortals is too much for her - I say goodbye.

I hold Maggie and wipe away her tears. "'Don't feel abandoned, I'm coming back. I'm only going because I have to, not because I want to."

"It's not fair." She means my children.

"Nothing is fair. I'm coming back as soon as I can."

July

I stay in London for less than a week.

Andy and the children want me to stay. I get more and more anxious. I am smoking forty cigarettes a day, and smell like an ashtray. Andy finds me in tears on our garden steps.

"Of course you must go then."

"I am so afraid she will die without me."

We telephone Italy but can only get hold of Viola. She can only tell me that Maggie is much, much worse.

"Male, male, piu male."

With more and more of a sense of urgency, I make arrangements for people to look after our children, clean the house, and pack again.

I phone again and finally get Marco.

"Maggie want to come home. Hattie is no longer at the 'ospital Maggie alone and very scared. She hallucinating. She tell us that terrible things are happening. They kidnap people from the hospital at night and kill them."

"Well, I'm coming over tomorrow."

"You're not!"

"I am."

"Well, Anita, we'll talk then."

*

My plane lands in the early evening. This time it is Luca who comes to meet me. Luca is Rhoda's husband, and Rhoda is Maggie's best friend in Italy.

"Maggie is home now. When we tell her you are coming she put her arms out as if she sees you already."

*

Maggie is downstairs where the dining table used to be. Her back is to me and she is surrounded by people.

"Anita is here," someone says.

Maggie turns. She raises her hands to ward me off.

"Don't touch me."

Her whisper is a shriek.

*

In less than a week, Maggie's essentialness blurred, and she has moved beyond my grasp. My connection to her was broken when I left. Her eyes have sunk back into her head and like an idiot child, she stares past me at nothing. Her belly is huge. Bedsores have appeared on her face and arms, and on her hips, they are soft, purple craters. Baby nappies are tucked around her bottom and in between her emaciated legs. Her feet are swollen, and she is covered in an icy, oily sweat.

I don't know what to do. The time for a soothing massage is gone. Maggie is in terrible pain. I sit down next to her on the stone-flagged floor and wait for my cue - any clues to show me what I can do for her.

*

The room is so full of people. Marco and Maria. Gia from next door. Lorenzo and Bianca from across the road. Rhoda and Luca. Gia bites back her tears.

Rhoda is nervous:

"When I got here this morning, Maggie insisted on having a bath, and wouldn't you know? There was no water. But she wouldn't give up. So we had to all go to neighbors with buckets, and bring back hot water for her. Bless her, she wanted to be clean. We said it didn't matter, but she was stubborn. Marco and Mateo put her into the bath with her nightie on, and cut it off, so as to move her as little as possible."

Rhoda waves her hands about, and steps from side to side. Accidentally, she bumps into the bed.

"Get away from there. Get away," snaps Maggie in a loud voice.

Rhoda is mortified, and tears fill her eyes.

"I'm sorry Maggie, I'm sorry. Yer old friend is a clumsy cow."

"I'm sorry - I'm sorry Rhoda."

"Think no more of it my dear. Think no more of it."

"I'm sorry - I'm sorry."

They all reassure her in English and Italian.

"I'm sorry."

"No, Maggie no. Va bene."

*

So many people come in and out. So many meals stood in the kitchen. So many cigarettes. Maria does no more housework. She stands alone in the garden - like a tree.

Afraid she'll slip away in the night; we refuse to sleep away from her. It works out better, because on the couch next to her bed, Marco knows he can let unconsciousness take him for an hour or so. A light from a small lamp falls onto her face. Shadows loom across its rim and invade her face in hollows. I drip medication into her mouth.

There is not enough flesh on her top lip to cover her teeth and she cannot swallow. We use a dropper to drip the medicine into her mouth. It takes four hours to give her a dose, and then it is time for another one. Always restless, she plucks at the white sheet that covers her.

Her nails have grown long, and her gold ring hangs on her wedding finger. "Marco," she calls out, "I hurt."

So we give her a morphine injection. We have no idea what we are doing.

Again, Marco has to look for a doctor who will come to the house and help us, but no one will come.

"She must go back into 'ospital," he says. But none will take her. Then he goes to look for a mortician.

We are all terrified of her pain.

*

Night again. Bedside light, low and orange.

Bianca, from across the road bursts in - sobs and shakes with terror. She wrings her hands and weeps. Her son Emilio has been in a road accident, and he has been taken to hospital. Her husband Lorenzo doesn't dare to go. He stays at home, stunned.

Mateo goes to find out the worst, and I give her a brandy. We wait in a tense silence. In the dark, cars speed by the house. I drip medication into Maggie's mouth.

When Mateo returns, he is wreathed in smiles. Bianca weeps for joy and goes to tell Lorenzo. The boy only has a few surface scratches and a mild concussion.

*

Maggie's friends come to visit. Often, they sit outside, and I go and sit with them. The garden is in full bloom.

Maria has put out pots of busy lizzie, and geraniums all along the side of the drive and in the porch where spiders have built webs in the corners, their silver patterns swaying in the breeze. House Martins have made nests in the eaves. They swoop in and out of the porch, and their young wheeze a welcome.

Lorenzo comes over from time to time, just to squat outside the front door on his haunches and smoke a cigarette. He only comes in if invited, and often goes to be with Maria in her garden.

I ask him about his son in my minimal Italian.

"Come va Emilio?"

"Bene, bene. Grazie."

"Bianca una femma bella."

"Si." He nods. "Piu calma."

*

Maggie has developed odd mannerisms. She grasps with her arms, as if she can put them around someone who lies on top of her. She smiles, but the pain makes it into more of a grimace. She wets her lips with her tongue. Then she grasps again and smiles.

"Anita." She calls my name. It is the first time she has asked for me.

I go over to her bed.

"Yes Maggie, I'm here."

"I love you." She mouths the words with care. "But it's very difficult."

She nods her head slowly, careful not to jog herself.

*

One afternoon, Marco turns her. He has to do this to give air to her bed sores and she can't do it for herself. Her mouth is pulled back from her teeth, and her eyes wide with fear. His face is right next to hers and in her extremity she snaps her mouth shut, biting him on his cheek.

"Owa!"

"I'm sorry, I'm sorry."

"Is okay Maggie." He rubs his cheek. "Is quite okay."

"I'm sorry, I'm sorry."

"Is okay Maggie. Don' worry."

When she is settled down again, she says to Marco with her new infinite care:

"You know, I'm really quite keen on you."

He is amused. "Why thank you Maggie, I'm quite keen on you too."

*

By five o'clock I have managed to get all of Maggie's medication into her. One drop, every five breaths. I have done well. Her next dose is not due until seven. The room is full of shadows. The night is a vast, empty sea. I am afraid. She is quiet, so I curl up on the flagstones at the foot of her bed, to snatch a couple of hours. At dawn Marco wakes me as he humps in a mattress for me to lie on.

*

Mateo has found a water pistol and squirts it at everybody - insistent and unstoppable. He jumps out from behind doors and drenches everyone. He squirts it several times into my face and I very nearly lose my temper - but I don't. This is his grief.

*

It is very hot and humid. Maria begins to fuss.

"'She cannot die here; it is too hot." She sends Mateo to find an air conditioner.

When he returns, it is with his girlfriend Bianca.

The air conditioner belongs to her. They arrive in her smart, little car and carry it past Maggie and I, into a little bedroom at the back of the house.

Bianca's air conditioner drives me into impotent rage and grief: rage for Maggie who is being treated like meant - dead meat; grief for myself, a different kind of meat - old meat: At the same moment that Maggie becomes a refrigeration problem, I enter into middle age.

*

Maria bustles about setting up the little room, preparing for Maggie's corpse. The air conditioner does its work, and the room is soon chilled and ready. But Maggie keeps us waiting.

*

Maria and Marco come in on each end of a pine bed. They have taken off the mattress and draped it in a white sheet. They put it down next to Maggie's bed.

Then, Maria sends Marco upstairs to get one of her outfits, for when she is laid out.

"This one is her favorite." He holds up a scarlet silk trouser suit and lays it on the white sheet still on its hanger. Then he looks for a headscarf to match from the table at the head of Maggie's bed.

"Marco, I think it would be better if you did all this in the other room."

He looks surprised. "Okay Anita."

It sounds cruel but it was not. We all have our obsessions, and Maria's was to be prepared and ready.

They pick up the bed with Maggie's things on it, and angle it back out again.

*

The change comes at nine o'clock. Leant against the wall with a cigarette, I have my eye on Maggie. As usual, the room is full of people. Bruno on the couch next to Lorenzo. Bianca in and out. Mateo and Maria cooking in the kitchen. Marco stood at the foot of her bed.

I see that Maggie is trying to look out of her face and see panic flaring in her eyes that she has managed to pull together. She begins to choke. Lorenzo helps me lift her higher onto her pillows. She coughs. I say the first thing that comes into my head.

"Don't be frightened Maggie, everything is all right."

Marco takes Lorenzo's place. "That's right Maggie. Don't be scared. Is okay."

Her desperate look relaxes a little, and she sighs, a long moaning sound.

"Aaaaaaaaaah."

"That's right" says Marco.

I moan with her – the same long "Aaaaaaaaah."

She responds and moans again. "Aaaaaaaaah." No more words.

"Try to relax Maggie. Don't fight it."

Again she reaches out through her eyes, and moans a high note, asking a question.

Again I say the first thing that comes into my head.

"Don't worry Maggie. It's just like having a baby, except that at the end of it, you give birth to yourself."

She relaxes completely then – lets her eyes go apart and settles down, like a woman in labor.

She sighs and moans, and, with each exhalation we join her. We breathe in with her and then breathe out again with the same sigh or moan. Mateo joins us. We match our pitch with hers, high or low, question or relief.

Sometimes she needs to cough. We cough with her and clear our throats, too.

Marco, Mateo and I join her on this human wind.
In and out, all four of us sigh and sing in Death.

*

Maggie looks at me, her lungs rattling. She has managed to pull her eyes together again so she can look at me.

This is it. But it is like watching her slowly drown.

I lean into her. "It's okay Maggie, just let go. We won't be far behind. You're just going first, is all."

"That's right. Soon you can run again, jus' like you used to."

"Well done Maggie, well done."

Marco and I hold her head, a hand on either cheek, our faces inches away.

"Well done, Maggie, well done."

My hand is on her cheek, my eyes on hers and like a kite broken free in the wind the life goes out of them. A cloud covers the deep inner landscape that is Maggie. They don't lose their brilliance, but they are dead eyes.

*

Mateo bursts into tears and runs from the room. Maria bursts into tears. Marco rubs his eyes with the heels of his hands.

"We must hurry, Anita, and get her ready."

Maria binds Maggie's jaw shut with one of her bandannas and we pull her into a sitting position. Maggie gives one last sigh.

"That's right Maggie. You take her head Anita." They start to pull off her sweat drenched clothes.

"Why don't you just cut them off?"

Marco rummages about for some scissors, and then exposes Maggie's emaciated, yet bloated body. As he cuts away her nightie and vest, we can all see her little girl's fanny, smooth and without hair. A pointed, purple swelling sticks out of her groin. Her breasts are crumpled and empty. She is smudged all over with bed sores.

Aching with love for her - I climb onto the bed behind her and lean her shoulders against my knees. She is still hot and feverish. I hold her head between my hands, crouched behind her, like a chair.

They dress her in her scarlet trousers and a red and white silk blouse. When they are finished, Marco and Mateo carry her into the air-conditioned room and I follow them holding onto her head, so it doesn't dangle. When she is settled, her clothes straight, and her hands crossed on her breast, they put a clean bandana on her head. Maria argues with Marco about how this should be done.

I sit on the floor behind her head and curl my hands around her cheeks to hold her eyes shut.

"We must call her mother."

"Would you like me to do it?"

"Yes Anita. You do it."

*

Telephones that ring after midnight sound different from telephones that ring in the day.

"Hello." Mildred knows what I am going to say.

"Mildred? This is Anita. It is all over."

She weeps. "I'm glad. She will have no more pain now."

"No. No more pain. It's all over."

"Well, thank you for calling Anita."

"It's all right. Goodbye."

"Goodbye."

The line clicks and then hisses. I put the phone down, and to my surprise find that I can't breathe.

I am alone in the upstairs main bedroom, so I sit on the bed and gasp for air - as if I can never get enough – as if there isn't enough air in the universe to satisfy me.

I feel myself separate into several different personalities and one of them is definitely having trouble breathing.

Another one feels a huge ebullient joy, and yet another is quite sorry for me. Another one still, doesn't think that this is genuine and is disapproving.

I cross to the window and open it. The smell of night comes in.

Marco comes upstairs to see what is taking so long and turns on the light to find me gasping for air.

"I'm fine."

Marco calls for Mateo and everyone comes upstairs.

"This is ridiculous," says the disapproving me. "Pull yourself together."

"I'm fine, I'm fine."

I wish they'd go away and leave me alone.

"Lie down." Mateo pushes me back onto the bed and begins to massage my stomach. Another me appears in order to be embarrassed and pissed off.

I lie on the bed and gasp in an emotional hall of mirrors. But my overriding sense is one of joy. A joy too great to hold in my lungs.

"It's a reaction." I hear someone say.

"Really?" thinks another, more scientific me. "How interesting. This must be hysteria."

"I'm fine, I'm fine."

Suddenly a wave of pure rage, hits me from behind, scattering all the little me' like a bag of dropped marbles. . It comes with such force, it pushes me off the bed in one wailing bound.

I flip onto my feet screaming with rage, spit dripping out of my mouth. I scream out of the window at God, who is just too small to account for this and I scream for the Devil who might be just about the right size. I want to face the source of this — kill it, murder it, stab it in the eyes, make it suffer. I'm in just the right mood to face down Beelzebub himself.

Someone holds me. It is Mateo.

"Okay Anita," he says, "show us your lovely bottom."

Behind me, I hear Marco.

"Yes Anita, we finally goin' to see your lovely bottom."

I turn in Mateo's arms, to find a very young, very scared looking doctor next to me with a syringe in one hand, and a swab of cotton wool in the other.

Tap-like my scream turns off.

I take the hand with the syringe in it and sit back down on the bed.

"All I need is for someone to hold my hand. I'm fine."

"My God' says Mateo, "Wha' you like when you are not fine?"

*

"Come downstairs now, Anita, and be with us."

We all troop back down and go into the room where Maggie is laid out. The doctor writes the death certificate in an atmosphere of carnival. Everyone smiles. They laugh and joke' glad that Maggie's ordeal is over.

I smile too and sit next to her on her hard pine bed. Most of her body is still warm, but her crossed hands are cold, and her face is set.

Maggie looks very different now. If I was seeing her for the first time - if I hadn't gone through her illness with her, it would be a great shock.

Only her nose, hands and feet look recognizable. Her identity passed away with her.

*

All the neighbors go home, and I sit next to Maggie, my hand around her waist, with Marco, Mateo and Bruno. Marco opens a bottle of brandy, and we all get drunk.

"She didn't know how good she was," says Marco.

But it is her stubbornness and irritability that please us the most – her constant criticizing that makes us laugh the most.

I get into a drunken argument with the men. Luca has the floor.

"In business you cannot have Bushido. It is not possible to have a code of honor like the Samurai. In Italy everyone try to fuck you, so you have to fight back. You cannot be sincere; you have to tell lies."

"Is true," says Mateo, "You have to work like a pig for nothing. Bushido is dead."

"Rubbish," I yell over Maggie's corpse. "All you've got is your word. The more money that is at stake, the more your word counts. Businessmen have to practice Bushido. If they lie to one another, no one dares to do business with them, anywhere in the world."

"No, no you are wrong." They are outraged. They think I am blind.

"You think Bushido keeps you safe from theft and fraud. But it doesn't because bad men practice Bushido too. Do you honestly think all the Samurai were good men? They treated their serfs like shit!"

"No. No."

Marco feels sick.

'I have to go to bed now. Tomorrow is a big day'.

We turn out the light and leave Maggie alone in the dark. Marco and Mateo go upstairs, and Luca leaves.

*

With nowhere left to sleep I climb into Maggie's bed, still damp with her sweat, and cry myself into a drunken sleep. Just before unconsciousness takes me, I shoot out into deep space full of filaments of light. These are not stars, but tendrils of brightness stretching into infinity.

A voice whispers in my ear, "depth", and I realize that I have never really heard that word before.

*

I wake up in the middle of a bustle. Aurelio is here. He sits on the couch and smiles at me out of his dark eyes.

"Buongiorno Signora."

"Buongiorno." I sit up in Maggie's bed, dazed with a hangover.

"He say Maggie visit him last night." Says Marco. "Always people visit him when they are dead. They go to Aurelio first."

"Oh."

I get up and go into Maggie. A ghost of warmth remains on her waist, where my hand lay last night. Otherwise, she is cold and silent. I kiss her good morning and startle back. I hear breathing. Very faint and shallow. But there can be no question. She is dead.

"Will you put make up on her, Anita?"

"Of course."

I dress in the bathroom and pick up both our make-up bags. She always liked to look her best.

Her face is marble, but her lips, when I paint them with a lip brush, give a little. I don't want to bend too close, because when I do, I can still hear faint breathing. I put pale grey shadow on her eyes, and peach powder under her cheek bones. Kiss her quickly and leave.

*

All day people stream in. They stand next to her and talk about, or to her. Some are tearful. Some are grave. But they are all glad that her ordeal is over. Then they go for refreshment. The men go to admire Maria's garden, and chat under the fruit trees drinking wine. The women cluster in the kitchen and talk. I am amazed by how many people came. How quickly the news of Maggie's death has spread. There was no time to tell anyone how ill she was. Her illness was too demanding.

A woman from the bar up the road says something that is translated for me:

"She would always say: "You look so tired." She was always so sympathetic."

*

Marco has arranged her funeral for tomorrow.

Although Maggie wants to be cremated, he has decided that she must be buried up the road in the local graveyard, so that Daisy and Chloe have somewhere to visit.

*

In the evening the undertakers come and put her into a coffin. I come in just as they are spraying her with a kind of air-freshener that smells of cinnamon. Maria places a small teapot at Maggie's feet. Maggie had been proud of it and jealous of it ever breaking. Marco takes off the lid and puts a photo of her and her children inside.

Birds sing and the swallow chicks wheeze.

*

The funeral is today. Everyone is tense, getting dressed in their best clothes and polishing shoes. I stand next to Maggie at a loose end.

Marco comes in with an English Bishop who is to do the ceremonies. Some of Maggie's English friends found him in Venice.

"How do you do. You are Mrs. Moretti's friend?"

"Yes. How do you do."

"It was very good of you to come so far, and leave your own family to be with her. You must have been very good friends indeed."

"Yes, we were."

"She must have been very brave to endure her illness. I have had cancer myself, and I know something of what she must have been through."

He blesses Maggie and then it is time to go. I kiss her one last time. The undertakers talk together which is a relief because over their low voices, I can't possibly hear Maggie's ghost breathing.

She is beginning to smell. Maria was right to be worried. They wrap her in the gauze that lines her coffin and she floats inside the small, white space before they put on the heavy lid, and screw it down. Then the undertakers pick her up and take her outside.

The Bishop leads us outside, behind her coffin. The garden is overflowing with local people, openly weeping, who have come to see her on her way. I get into a car with Marco and Mateo, and we follow Maggie in silence to the church.

The churchyard is full of people. A bell tolls, and shuts out the sound of birds. The air resounds and Marco has to mime to me, what he wants me to do. He wants me to walk, directly behind Maggie, with him, into the church behind her. A great honor.

I hold Marco's arm. It is tense and masculine, and he squeezes my hand, his face expressionless behind dark glasses. Men take Maggie up onto their shoulders, and I follow behind, down the center aisle, past the pews, filled with people, on their feet and still, as they watch us pass by.

I don't remember the sermon, nor the prayers. Because I am back in Guernsey with Maggie, and it is she who sits next to me - instead of Marco.

*

We are trying not to fidget. We sit next to my grandmother who listens to the sermon, her head tilted, and her hands crossed in her lap. I look at the sun as it comes through a stained-glass window of a lily with a ribbon that says: *He called a little child unto him.*

Maggie looks ahead at a brass vase full of red carnations and sprays of greenery. I know she is counting the flowers. Beside us, red and blue light from the window glows on the wooden pew. It has moved about three inches since we arrived.

Outside, high in the air above the steeple, the faint call of seagulls. Sunbeams waft with incense. We are hungry.

At last, it is time to sing, and with a rumble and a few coughs, the congregation gets to its feet.

The rector walks behind a cross carried by an altar boy, and behind him, in pairs, the choir, and last, the chaplain, with the collection on a brass plate. The organ hums with the refrain from the last hymn. This is the most difficult bit.

Our dignity won't let us move a muscle. When they have gone, my grandmother kneels to say goodbye to God until next Sunday, and we copy her, and bow our heads into our hands. Then my grandmother gathers her books, the signal for us to stop our prayers, and she gets to her feet, and opens the catch, of the pew door.

Hello, Mu, how are you my dear? And she is swept off with one of her bridge cronies. We follow behind, and out the door into the sunshine of the churchyard. We skip on the gravel that scrunches with feet and walking sticks.

Is this Nita? How she has grown!

And little Margaret. My goodness how time flies!

*

Time for the burial ground now. Maggie is put into the hearse, and there is the usual kerfuffle about who gets into whose car. People chatter about the service – the flowers and how Maggie would have liked it and so on. I get back into Marco's car and we drive slowly in procession to the cemetery. The church bell tolls.

The whole of Oriago has downed tools. A wheelbarrow with a hoe in it is left in the middle of a field. The canal that winds its way along the road seems to have stopped. The land is green and flying with insects. The sky is milk.

As we drive past Maggie's house, Maria waits to wave, and Georgia, Maggie's dog, barks wildly.

There is no traffic and no noise.

At the graveyard, people gather round a hole in the ground, and more and more arrive. Larks sing. The ground shimmers and heat trapped in the earth comes back up through my espadrilles. The service is short.

I wake up when Maggie is being lowered into the cool interior of her grave. When it is time to throw sods of earth onto her coffin, I can't. She wanted to be confined to fire, and the sea of home. So, instead I throw in a blue hydrangea — like the ones that grew in my grandmother's garden.

*

To get away from all the people, I cross the road to walk beside the canal. I pass through the long grass, disturbing the insects and small butterflies.

On the small wooden pier for the boats, it is very hot, so I go down the bank and get into the canal. I sing songs that Maggie would have liked to the opposite shore. It seems reasonable enough. My feet sink into mud, and the water swirls around my waist.

After a while, Mateo comes with a friend to look for me.

"Is time for lunch, Anita. We eat in the house next door. Gia have made food for us."

"OK, I'll be along soon."

"You all right?"

"Yes. I'll be along. Don't worry."

"OK Anita, we see you soon."

I lie down in the water. It has been an ordeal.

*

When I walk back for the inevitable meal, a hot wind dries my dress. At the back of Maria's vegetable garden, I go through a little gate and cross a courtyard into the next door house. The front door is open, and inside, I can hear voices and laughter. I cross a couple of big empty rooms and find myself in the dining room. Many people are around a long wooden table, laden with good food and wine.

"Come on, Anita," yells Marco, "We have food for you."

I sit down opposite Aurelio who is enjoying Grappa and company. Everyone shouts and flirts in Italian.

Aurelio interrupts them all to talk at length. He looks at me with tears in his eyes and waves his beautiful hands.

Mateo translates: "He say you do not touch his back for luck, like so many people do. You do not make him feel like he has a hunched back. You treat him like everyone else. You treat him like a man. He say that when he see you with Maggie, he can see that you think a lot. He can see that you think about things. He like you. He say many nice things about you. Bu' you don't need to know. You know already."

*

It is obvious that I must go. The family needs to clump together in order to heal.

Marco leaves for the seaside. He has to break the news to Daisy and Chloe. His next ordeal.

I stay a few days, alone with Maria, because there is no flight for a week. By myself, I walk along the canal, visit Maggie's grave, or sit in the garden smoking cigarettes.

On the day I leave, Marco comes back from the beach to see me off. He looks less tired now.

"What are you going to do now, Marco?"

"Wha' do you mean?"

"I mean, how are you going to look after the children and work as well?"

"My mother and Viola will stay with us. They will look after the children. Maggie, the bitch, has landed me right in it." He smiles.

I smile too. "All alone in a house full of women."

"Si. They will all break my balls." He is silent for a moment.

"I wish I took Maggie to more parties. She loved parties and I never want to go. But she did love a party."

I have no more to say.

It is hard to part in the middle of an airport milling with tourists.

Marco leaves me at passport control. He pinches my cheek hard and leaves without looking back.

Elegy

If I could take you home
to where the sea swells, against
the steep and ringing shore
I would.

If I could take you home
to where the sky holds the cloud
to its deep and windy heart,
I would.

If I could take you back
to that earth that dreamed
our roots together, I would.

If I could.
*   To childhood's morning*
of wet grass, secret, silver-trailing snails
and early birds. To where the horse snorts
the cow bellows and milk pails clatter and
the cock stalks the time-keeping sun.

Where we learnt the innocence of lavender
the intimate, pepper-smell of roses, the
summons of the brass doorbell, too hot
to touch and the sudden joy of the tea-kettles
shriek from the bottom of the garden.

In this place the shadows are long.

A starless midnight calls — a voice
with no echo.

Goodbye my bunny, my lovely dark girl.

*When I return, alone as I must,
I shall search for you in all those things
we lived — find you in everything
we became.*

www.ingramcontent.com/pod-product-compliance
Lightning Source LLC
Chambersburg PA
CBHW020928090426
42736CB00010B/1075